CREATING THE PATH
TO SUCCESS IN THE CLASSROOM

CREATING THE PATH TO SUCCESS IN THE CLASSROOM

Teaching to Close the Graduation Gap for Minority, First-Generation, and Academically Unprepared Students

Kathleen F. Gabriel

Foreword by Stephen Carroll

STERLING, VIRGINIA

Published by Stylus Publishing, LLC 22883 Quicksilver Drive
Sterling, Virginia 20166-2102

Library of Congress Cataloging-in-Publication Data
Names: Gabriel, Kathleen F. , author.
Title: Creating the path to success in the classroom : teaching to close
the graduation gap for minority, first-generation & academically
unprepared students / Kathleen F. Gabriel.
Description: First edition. |
Sterling, Virginia: Stylus Publishing, LLC., [2018] |
Includes bibliographical references.
Identifiers: LCCN 2017039310 (print) |
LCCN 2017059496 (ebook) |
ISBN 9781579225575 (Library networkable e-edition) |
ISBN 9781579225582 (Consumer e-edition) |
ISBN 9781579225568 (pbk. : alk. paper) |
ISBN 9781579225551 (cloth : alk. paper)
Subjects: LCSH: Minority college students--United States. |
First-generation college students--United States. |
Underprepared college students--United States. |
College teaching--United States. |
Teacher-student relationships--United States. |
Communication in education--United States. |
Mentoring in education--United States. |
College dropouts--United States--Prevention.
Classification: LCC LC3731 (ebook) |
LCC LC3731 .G325 2018 (print) |
DDC 378.1/982--dc23
LC record available at https://lccn.loc.gov/2017039310

13-digit ISBN: 978-1-57922-555-1 (cloth)
13-digit ISBN: 978-1-57922-556-8 (paperback)
13-digit ISBN: 978-1-57922-557-5 (library networkable e-edition)
13-digit ISBN: 978-1-57922-558-2 (consumer e-edition)

Printed in the United States of America

All first editions printed on acid-free paper
that meets the American National Standards Institute

Z39-48 Standard.

Bulk Purchases
Quantity discounts are available for use in workshops
and for staff development.
Call 1-800-232-0223

First Edition, 2018

This book is dedicated to Dean Dixon, retired Chico Senior High teacher and counselor. Dean, through his commitment, dedication, and passion to serve "underserved" students for more than 50 years, has been a true role model and inspiration to me and so many other educators.

CONTENTS

FOREWORD   xi
Stephen Carroll

1   RETENTION, PERSISTENCE, AND SUCCESS
     Clarifying the Challenge   1
     Introduction   1
     Institutional Response and Increased Expectations   6
     What Does Teaching Have To Do With This?   8
     Significance of the Teaching Professor   9
     Overview of the Chapters   10
     Conclusion   11
     Notes   12

2   CLASS CLIMATE
     Widening the Circle for a Diverse Student Body   13
     Introduction   13
     Promote a Positive Classroom Climate   14
     Embrace Students' Diversity   18
     Increase Our Own Cultural Competence   20
     Encourage Student Interactions   21
     Foster a Community of Learners Within Our Classes   23
     Conclusion   27

3   THE FIRST MONTH OF THE SEMESTER
     Engage, Connect, and Commit   29
     Introduction   29
     Class Protocols (or Policies)   30
     In-Class Engagement Expectations   31
     Importance of Making Connections   34
     Activating Prior Knowledge   35
     Increase Relevancy With Real-World Issues   37
     Culturally Relevant Material   38
     Significance of a Commitment   40
     Conclusion   41
     Notes   42

4   MOTIVATION AND ATTITUDES
     Impact of Mindsets and Mental Toughness Attributes   43
     Introduction   43
     Mindsets: Fixed or Growth   44

Promoting Growth Mindsets 46
Mental Toughness 50
Nurturing Mental Toughness Components 52
Self-Efficacy Reinforced 56
Conclusion 59
Note 59

5 INTERACTIVE LECTURES
Using Meaningful Educational Activities 61
Introduction 61
Favoritism and Bias of the Traditional Lecture Format 62
Creating Interactive Lectures 64
Improving Lecture Techniques 72
PowerPoints, Class Notes, and Handouts 75
Conclusion 78
Notes 78

6 READING ASSIGNMENTS AND CLASS DISCUSSIONS
Stimulate Deeper Learning 79
Introduction 79
Required Books: "Choose 'Em and Use 'Em" 80
Preparing for Class: Reflections and Responses 84
Anticipating Difficulty With the Reading: Five Steps to Use 88
Reading and Critical Thinking Skills 91
Conclusion 94
Note 94

7 WRITING ASSIGNMENTS
Promote Critical Thinking and Writing 95
Introduction 95
The Quintessential Value of the Written Word 96
In-Class Response Writing Tasks 97
Out-of-Class Reflective Writing Tasks 101
Substantive Formal Writing: Procrastination and Plagiarism 103
Discouraging Plagiarism and Encouraging Scrutiny of Sources 108
Conclusion 111
Notes 112

8 RESILIENCE, HABITS, AND PERSISTENCE
Hold Fast and See It Through 113
Introduction 113
Building Academic Resilience 115
Developing Positive Habits and Routines 118
Promoting Productive Persistence 121
Conclusion 126
Note 127

EPILOGUE
Final Thoughts
Teacher Impact on Diverse College Students   129

APPENDIX A
Readings for Expanding Cultural Competence   131

APPENDIX B
Organizing Student Interaction With Multiple Small-Group Configurations 135

APPENDIX C
**Quote of the Week: Examples From Diverse People for Supporting
Growth Mindsets and Mental Toughness Attributes**   139

APPENDIX D
Note-Taking Tips for Students and a Few Tips for Professors   145

APPENDIX E
A Strategy for Building Vocabulary   149

REFERENCES   153

ABOUT THE AUTHOR   169

INDEX   171

*C*reating the Path to Success in the Classroom: Teaching to Close the *Graduation Gap for Minority, First-Generation, and Academically Unprepared Students* is an even more significant book than it first appears to be. Kathleen Gabriel's new book joins Saundra McGuire's (2015) *Teach Students How to Learn* and Terry Doyle and Todd Zakrajsek's (2013) *The New Science of Learning* on the top tier of books focused on enhancing student learning and success in college, and that makes it noteworthy. But this book is more than just a standout contribution to a vital and rapidly growing field. Gabriel's argument that good teaching is the best way to meet the diverse needs of today's college students is an idea whose time has come on many levels.

The size and heterogeneity of the college student body has been increasing for decades. In 1960 only 45% of American high-school graduates enrolled in college; in 2009 70% went on to college. According to the National Center for Education Statistics (NCES) (2016), the percentage has hovered between 66% and 69% since then. The European-based Organisation for Economic Co-operation and Development (OECD) (2017), using a slightly different method of calculation, puts the number slightly above 80%. *Inside Higher Education* (Kovacs, 2016) adds that, "nearly 90 percent of millennials who graduate from high school attend college within eight years." Any way you look at it, the increase is huge. The percentage of the population that goes to college is now bigger than it has ever been. But the percentage increases alone don't tell the full story, because they've been magnified by a rapidly rising population. In 1960, 3.6 million Americans enrolled in college. By 1980, that number had had more than tripled to over 12 million. In 2000, it was 15.3 million, and in 2017, 20.4 million. Since the turn of the century, we have added nearly twice as many college students as there were in the whole country in 1960 (NCES, 2016b, Table 303.30).

These increases have not been evenly distributed. In 1960, 54% of men who completed high school went on to college, whereas only 38% of women did the same (NCES, 2016b, Table 302.10). Now female graduates are more likely than males to enroll in college, 73% to 66% (NCES, 2016b, Table 302.10). In 1972, 38.4% of Black and 50% of Hispanic high-school graduates went on to college. In 2015, those numbers were 62.6% and 67.1%

respectively (NCES, 2016b, Table 302.20). Between roughly the same dates, the percentage of White college students fell from 84% to 58% (NCES, 2016b, Table 306.10). In 1975, 34.7% of low-income high-school graduates enrolled in college. In 2015, 63.1% did (NCES, 2016b, Table 302.30). Finally, the number of students aged 25 and older enrolling in college rose 16% from 2004 to 2014, and the percentage of nontraditional students continues to rise (NCES, 2016a). Today, almost 30% of college students are over 25 years old (NCES, 2016b, Table 303.50) and over 73% meet at least one qualifier for nontraditional status according to NCES (NCES, 2015).

These enormous increases and dramatic demographic shifts mean that large numbers of students who in years past would never have attended college are now sitting in our classrooms. In previous decades, college students tended to be mostly White, male, and economically affluent, but the students entering our classes are increasingly diverse across an increasing number of axes: gender, race/ethnicity, age, socioeconomic status, mental health/ learning abilities, levels of preparation, and more. To serve those students at least as well as we have served those in previous generations thus calls for a new pedagogy—a pedagogy that can accommodate not only the vast differences between past generations of students and today's but also the increasing differences between one class and the next and even between sections of the same class.

This is exactly what Gabriel's new book does. In chapter 1, she argues that the teaching faculty are the single most important factor in all students' success in college and that for minority, low-income, first-generation, and academically at-risk students, our role is even more critical because we are their primary role models, points of contact, and faces of the institution. Thus, it is incumbent upon us to adopt learning-centered pedagogies that maximize students' opportunities for success. In chapter 2, she then outlines a number of ways that professors can improve classroom climate and interaction with students—especially nontraditional students. In chapter 8, Gabriel shows us how to create psychological environments and classroom practices that build students' resilience, persistence, and other habits and mindsets conducive to long-term success. Throughout, Gabriel's pedagogy models and fosters deep appreciation for students' diversity and focuses relentlessly on using that diversity to improve education for all students using research-proven tools and techniques.

We know from recent research—pioneered notably by Elaine Seymour (2000) and others—that the best way to raise the learning performance of *all* students is by improving teaching. Repeated ethnographic studies have demonstrated conclusively that when teaching improves, everyone benefits, but the learning of traditionally underrepresented, underprepared, and otherwise disadvantaged students benefits the most. This research functions as the major premise that underlies this entire book. Gabriel's pedagogy is deeply rooted in the principles of universal design, which is to say that it is based on the fundamental principles of how human beings learn. Her pedagogy builds on the skills, aptitudes, capabilities, and facilities shared by all human beings by virtue of their common humanity. Thus, her work builds on the most current research on teaching and learning to offer a pedagogy that is not just human, but also humane. Gabriel offers detailed and empathetic accounts of (usually unintended) obstacles to student learning in chapters 3, 5, 6, and 7 and then offers solutions that professors can implement to help students overcome those obstacles. Chapter 3 is particularly valuable because it connects several principles central to modern learning theory (learning is making connections, engagement and relevance are crucial to managing attention, commitment is necessary for long-term learning, etc.) to classroom climate, policies, protocols, and practices.

Gabriel's deep integration of theory and practice is another factor that makes *Creating the Path to Success in the Classroom* a timely, rare, and valuable book. As the influential composition teacher-scholar Ann Berthoff (1981) reminds us, theory and practice must engage each other dialectically. Theory informs and guides practice, making assessment and thereby (proof of) progress possible—and vice versa. Yet most books about teaching separate them, focusing primarily or entirely on one, while ignoring or downplaying the other. Thus, while books like Bransford, Brown, and Cocking's (2000) *How People Learn: Brain, Mind, Experience, and School* and Ambrose, Bridges, DiPietro, Lovett, and Norman's (2010) *How Learning Works: Seven Research-Based Principles for Smart Teaching* help us understand learning on a theoretical level, and McKeachie and Svinicki's (2005) *Teaching Tips: Strategies, Research, and Theory for College and University Teachers*; Barkley's (2009) *Student Engagement Techniques: A Handbook for College Faculty;* and Angelo and Cross's (1993) *Classroom Assessment Techniques: A Handbook for College Teachers* help us develop more effective teaching practices, when theory and practice are separated like this, in the words of Ann Berthoff (1981), "practice gets gimmicky and theory becomes dogmatic" (p. 35). Gabriel's book, however, integrates theory and practice in each chapter and explicitly discusses how they inform and constrain each other. Chapter 5 on interactive lectures showcases this integration especially well. Gabriel starts with the historical origins of the lecture and the conditions which led to its widespread acceptance and propagation. She then provides a detailed theoretical account of the advantages and disadvantages of lecturing before delving into the research on how lecturing (including active lecturing) affects student learning. She derives some basic principles from both the theories and the research and then builds a detailed, step-by-step model for constructing effective, active lectures. The practice derives from the theory. But at the end of the exposition of this model, Gabriel includes a few sections on techniques for improving lectures which are drawn largely from practice. In her explorations of these practices, she notes how research into these techniques has fed back into and informed theory. Her chapters model the dialectical codependence of theory and practice elegantly. This deep and persistent integration makes her book far more useful than those which focus on one or the other, because it keeps theory accessible and practice extensible. When you understand the theory that informs a practice or exercise, you can figure out how to fix it when it doesn't work the way you want it to; you can discern what comes next; you can develop and ramify it; and you can adapt it to new situations, new classes, and new kinds of students. Thus, Gabriel encourages teachers of all types, from the newest to the most experienced, to adapt her practices and pedagogies to the unique environments and diverse students of their own classrooms, making her pedagogy their own and facilitating the success of all students in all those classrooms.

Finally, Gabriel's book teaches us a most important lesson that nearly everyone who works in this space misses: Because today's college students are so diverse—and diverse in ways that are not immediately apparent—teaching well requires us to teach them how to do *everything* they need to do to succeed. In the past, we could count on students knowing how to read, take notes, annotate, study, take tests, write papers, and so on. No more. Now we know students need to be taught how to do all these things and more. Students need to be taught how to behave in classrooms, how to manage their emotions, how to manage their time, how to be engaged. Gabriel's book shows us how to do all of these things. Equally important, Gabriel reminds us that we too might need to relearn some things. She gently but persistently insists that by connecting with and investing ourselves in our students; by creating welcoming, supportive learning environments; by enabling and expecting our students to grow into their best selves; and by taking responsibility for the learning and success of *all* our students, we have the power to reshape our society, increasing opportunity, increasing equality, increasing justice, and increasing freedom for everyone. It's a book—and a message—that should inspire us all.

Stephen Carroll, PhD
Senior Lecturer, Department of English
Santa Clara University

RETENTION, PERSISTENCE, AND SUCCESS

Clarifying the Challenge

Education remains the key to both economic and political empowerment.

—*Barbara Jordan (1936–1996)*

Introduction

Every fall, with high hopes, millions of new students in the United States begin the daunting journey of attending college in pursuit of a college degree. However, only about half will achieve this mission. For more than 30 years, colleges and universities have struggled to improve their graduation rates while maintaining their academic standards. Yet, graduation rates have essentially remained stagnant (Habley, Bloom, & Robbins, 2012; Seidman, 2012; Tinto, 2012).

To make improvements for students, colleges and universities have examined and reformed various aspects of college life including housing, financial support, student affairs services, academic support, and advisory services (Seidman, 2012). However, the vital role that professors play in impacting graduation results often receives less attention. The fact is that students' success and, ultimately, their graduation are directly tied to their academic records.

As professors, we can have a tremendous impact on students' engagement, learning, and academic success. The purpose of this book is therefore to examine numerous ways we can create pathways for success in our classes and classrooms, especially for those who, traditionally, have had the lowest success rates in college: minority, first-generation (including low-income), and academically unprepared students. By examining our teaching methods and the impact we have on our students' learning and involvement in our courses, we can actively participate in students' academic performance in college, which is a major indicator of student success (Perna & Thomas, 2006).

The Impact of Education, Especially Higher Education

The importance of "getting an education" has been an integral part of our American heritage. Our second president, John Adams, wrote in 1785,

> The Whole People must take upon themselvs [sic] the Education of the Whole People and be willing to bear the expenses of it. There should not be a district of one Mile Square without a school in it, not founded by a Charitable individual but maintained at the expense of the People themselvs [sic].

Thomas Jefferson also noted that people needed to be educated in order to have a democratic, self-governed society. In 1787, he advised, "Educate and inform the whole mass of the people . . . . They are the only sure reliance for the preservation of our liberty." While our forefathers lived at a time when higher education institutions were not available for most people other than the affluent, they supported and promoted the widespread availability of public education for elementary and secondary students.

By the late nineteenth and early twentieth centuries, high schools became a very important part of the educational landscape, and the number of young people attending colleges was growing. By this time, higher education opportunities were far greater in the United States than in any European country (Colby, Ehrlich, Beaumont, & Stephens, 2003). In keeping with what our founding fathers believed about the importance of education, President Franklin D. Roosevelt (1938) noted, "Democracy cannot succeed unless those who express their choice are prepared to choose wisely. The real safeguard of democracy, therefore, is education."

Recognizing education's vital role in the preparation of citizens in a democratic society, Astin (1999a) clarifies that "our colleges and universities educate each new generation of leaders in government, business, science, law, medicine, the clergy, and other advanced professions, and train the personnel who will educate the entire citizenry at the precollegiate level" (p. 8). Therefore, what we do as professors in "educating" our students is of utmost importance not just for students' personal welfare, but also for our democratic society.

The term *professors* does not refer to only those who teach at four-year colleges and universities. Community colleges are also educating students and offering job training to assist them in contributing to their communities. Higher education is fundamental for "providing effective learning experiences [that are] critical for both the students themselves and our society, which increasingly relies on every individual to participate productively in our economy, our democracy, and the global village" (McClenney, 2004, p. 3).

In today's society, many believe that a college education is also necessary for a person "to be economically self-sufficient and deal effectively with the increasingly complex social, political, and cultural issues of the twenty-first century" (Kuh, Kinzie, Buckley, Bridges, & Hayek, 2007, p. 1). Kuh, Kinzie, and colleagues (2007) add, "Earning a baccalaureate degree is the most important rung in the economic ladder" (p. 1). Regarding future employment, according to the American Association of Community Colleges (2012), "by 2018, nearly two-thirds of all American jobs will require a post-secondary certificate or degree" (p. viii). In addition to fulfilling job requirements, having a degree significantly increases earning potential. The Social Security Administration's (2015) Office of Retirement Policy reports that "men with bachelor's degrees earn approximately $900,000 more in median lifetime earnings than high school graduates. Women with bachelor's degrees earn $630,000 more." Tinto (2012) points out that those who earn an associate's degree from a two-year college will have a lifetime working income that is "about $354,000 more than people who only complete high school" (p. 1). Thus, there are many benefits from earning a college degree, and economic empowerment is only one of them (Lee, 1999).

Every year, more and more students are enrolling in four-year colleges and universities, and the student population is more diverse than ever before in terms of socioeconomic backgrounds and ethnicities (Habley et al., 2012; National Center for Education Statistics, 2012b; Seidman, 2005a). This is also true for community colleges. "In 2000, about 5.5 million degree-seeking students attended two-year colleges. In the 2010–2011 school year, that number jumped to more than 8 million" (Koebler, 2012, p. 1). Despite recognizing the need for and importance of higher education for economic, political, and social reasons, too many of those who enroll in a college do not obtain a certificate or degree, or even complete more than a semester or two of college courses. Seidman (2012) notes, "Even though access to higher education is becoming universally available, many students who start in a higher education program drop out prior to completing a degree or achieving their individual academic and/or social goals" (p. 3).

These early exits come with "financial consequences . . . both for the student and for the college" (Seidman, 2012, p. 2). For many students, college loans are still looming, not to mention costs spent on tuition, books, housing, and so forth. Seidman (2012) found that for colleges the lost tuition revenue and monies spent on auxiliary services is also substantial. Beyond the monetary consequences that colleges, students, and their families might face when a student leaves, drops out, or is dismissed (flunks out), "on a broader societal level . . . we all have an interest promoting student success" (Gabriel, 2016, p. 178). Having an educated citizenship is vital to our democracy, our economy, and our culture.

Graduation Rates and Gaps Revealed

Across the nation, college graduation rates were not reported in a stand-ardized way until 1990 when Congress passed Public Law (P.L.) 101-542, commonly known as the Student Right-to-Know Act. This law created a standardized way for colleges and universities to report their graduation rates and mandates that all institutions eligible for Title IV funding "cal-culate completion or graduation rates of certificate- or degree-seeking, full-time students entering that institution" (National Center for Education Statistics, 2012a). The federal formula is based on the number of full-time freshman students who ultimately graduated from the institution where they initially enrolled within six years of initial enrollment. Now, even though there are critics of this basic formula, it does provide a consist-ent and standardized mechanism to compare graduation rates at different colleges and universities.

After P.L. 101-542 came into effect and graduation data were made pub-lic, early reports revealed that "at the typical institution, less than 40 percent of students earn their four-year degree in four years. Extending the time frame to six years brings the average institutional graduation rate up to roughly 57 percent" (Carey, 2008, p. 2). In the 1990s, for many educators and parents, this information was alarming. Yet, since that time, the overall graduation rates have stayed more or less the same. Hess, Schneider, Carey, and Kelly (2009) point out that the latest statistics reveal "on average, four-year colleges graduate fewer than 60 percent of their freshmen within six years. At many institutions, graduation rates are far worse" (p. 3). Specifically, in 2009,

> The University of Louisville . . . has a 44 percent six-year graduation rate. At the University of Memphis, the rate is 34 percent. The University of Alaska, Fairbanks, graduates only 25 percent of students within six years. Graduation rates below 50, 40, and even 30 percent are distressingly easy to find, even when the measure is the percentage of students graduating within six years. (Hess et al., 2009, p. 8)

As for community colleges, graduation rates are even lower. For 2-year public institutions, only 25% of those entering school "in 1995–96 with a goal of earning a degree or certificate had obtained . . . [a degree or a certifi-cate] at that institution by 2001, six years later" (McClenney, 2004, p. 5). Overall, whether examining 2- or 4-year colleges, the number of students starting college has increased but the percentage of those being able to stay, persist, and graduate has "remained relatively constant over the past five dec-ades" (Habley et al., 2012, p. 6).

The Right-to-Know data reports have also exposed the "graduation gap" among different ethnic and socioeconomic status (SES) groups. Throughout the country, "low-income students and students of color . . . complete college at especially low rates" (Offenstein, Moore, & Shulock, 2010, p. 1). When investigating the educational pipeline for low-income, African American, Latino, and Native American students, the "bad news" is that enrollment and persistence for these students and for students with disabilities "continues to lag behind [that of] White and Asian students" (Kuh, Kinzie, Buckley, Bridges, & Hayek, 2006, p. 1). For example, after 6 years, the graduation rates of the freshman cohort of 1995–2007 at 4-year Title IV institutions were as follows: 35.6% for American Indian/Alaska Native students, 38.5% for Black (non-Hispanic) students, and 43.5% for Hispanic students. However, the White (non-Hispanic) students had a much higher rate, 57.3%, and the rate for Asian/Pacific Islander students was even higher, 63% (Seidman, 2005b, p. 30).

The "gap" is similar when examining two-year community colleges. Opp (2002) found that "Hispanics, American Indians, Blacks, and Asian Americans were underrepresented in their Associate degree completion rates in comparison to their enrollment in the two-year college sector" (p. 148). In addition, Gabriel (2016) states, "Many did not even get close to earning a degree" (p. 177). Furthermore, according to the American Association of Community Colleges (2012), "For Hispanic, Black, Native American, and low-income students . . . nearly half of all community college students entering in the fall term drop out before the second fall term begins" (p. 9).

College professors, administrators, and researchers have also identified another category of students who have struggled in college. This group is often referred to as those who are academically unprepared or underprepared.[1] (This category can include students from other identified subgroups including minority, nonminority, and high to low income.) The retention and success "often translates into students failing to meet the academic challenges of adjusting to college life, especially those encountered during their freshman year. The adjustment is particularly difficult for underprepared freshmen—those who require remedial classes" (Grunder & Hellmich, 1996, p. 21). Engstrom (2008) also notes that the urban two- and four-year colleges that "serve large numbers of working-class and underrepresented students" (p. 6) have the greatest challenge of providing academic support for these students. "In those institutions, it is estimated that approximately 45 percent of beginning students participate in some form of academic support or basic skills courses" (Engstrom, 2008, p. 6). When studying the impact of students taking remedial classes, Kuh, Kinzie, Schuh, Whitt, and Associates (2005) found that "seventy percent of students who took at least one remedial reading course in college do not obtain a degree or certificate within eight years of enrollment" (p. 1). Thus, not only do many colleges have low graduation rates overall, but there are also significant disparities in retention and graduation rates among different groups, including ethnic and SES groups, within numerous colleges.

Institutional Response and Increased Expectations

The focus on retention and graduation rates did not come about just from the Right-to-Know law. From the 1960s to 1980s, college and university campuses were increasingly interested in student retention as an early sign and predictor of eventual graduation (Berger, Ramírez, & Lyons, 2012). Intervention programs, retention specialists, and tutoring centers were created in hopes of decreasing academic dismissals and student dropout or withdrawal numbers, especially during the 1980s and 1990s. Within the last 30 years "the number of retention interventions has expanded dramatically" (Habley et al., 2012, p. 214). Nevertheless, "substantial gains in student retention have been hard to come by . . . . The national rate of student persistence and graduation has shown disappointingly little change" (Tinto, 2006–2007, p. 2).[2] When examining the data from 1983 to 2011, Habley and colleagues (2012) also found graduation rates basically "stagnant" (p. 230). Thus, improving these rates remains on the forefront of institutional challenges (Braxton, 2006; Tinto, 2006–2007).

Part of the recent focus has come from the fact that retention and graduation rates are now part of how colleges and universities are judged, ranked, and even evaluated. Furthermore, "retention is used as a key indicator of institutional effectiveness" (Seidman, 2012, p. 28). Many state legislatures now have regulations that "use some measure of institutional retention and/ or graduation rates in their accountability programs for state sponsored or supported institutions . . . . Even the Federal government is considering using institutional retention rates in a national system of higher educational accountability" (Tinto, 2006–2007, p. 5). The state of Florida provides an example where "accountability measures mandate, among other things, specific information about enrollment, persistence, and completion of degree programs. The state's newly implemented performance-based budgeting measures also appropriate monetary rewards to community colleges largely based on student degree completions" (Grunder & Hellmich, 1996, p. 28). Overall, because the data are accessible to students, parents, and the general public, the response has been strong. "Increasing student retention matters more now than ever" (Tinto, 2006–2007, p. 5).

Hess and colleagues (2009) point out that one easy way "to pad graduation rates is to drop standards and hand a diploma to every student who walks through the door" (p. 4). They (along with others) are also quick to indicate that this is a tactic that no college should take. Lowering standards is not a valid or sound option. Another approach that would most likely guarantee higher graduation rates is for institutions to be very selective and limitative in their admission process. After all, most universities that have highly selective admissions (e.g., Harvard, Yale, Stanford) have much higher than average graduation rates (Hess et al., 2009). However, these colleges and universities also offer limited access and have much less socioeconomic and ethnic diversity than other types of institutions (Tinto, 2006–2007).

Most other colleges and universities have a broader admission policy and believe that it is imperative for institutions of higher education to be accessible. First-generation students, low-income students, and those who are unprepared must have a chance to earn degrees or certificates because "promoting the cause of equity and maximizing the development of talent are fundamental purposes for all higher education institutions" (Astin, 1984, 1993, as cited in Opp, 2002, p. 161). Furthermore, having a diverse student population "is imperative to cultivate multiple perspectives and aid individuals' growth" (Lee, 1999, p. 10).

In today's society, some ask, "Must *everyone* go to college?" As a public middle and high school educator for 17 of my 35-plus years in teaching, my answer is, "Of course not." Some people simply have no desire to go to college, and some do not want to put in the time or incur the expense. Others find careers or employment that do not require a 4-year college degree. There are even some who are not willing to handle or are not capable of handling college-level work. Although it is still possible in our society—albeit much more difficult—for one to have a worthwhile career or job that does not require a certificate or college degree, we should not assume who can and cannot be successful in college, nor should struggling students be left to "figure out" on their own how to make it in college. Certainly, improving the college preparation students receive in high school is important, but we cannot (and should not) have a laissez-faire attitude about what happens after students enter college. Colleges and universities must continue to seek ways to create and support "conditions that foster student success" (Kuh, Kinzie, et al., 2007, p. 1).

When considering the many different factors that can affect student success, there are still "many unresolved issues" (Berger et al., 2012, p. 28). Carey (2008) summarizes the main difference between the colleges and universities that have improved retention and graduation rates and closed the gap among different student groups and those that have not. He believes failure prevails "because at many institutions the success of undergraduates, particularly those from disadvantaged backgrounds, is not the priority it should be" (p. 1). Among all of our colleges and universities, we can and must do better. Tinto and Pusser (2006) suggest that we need research on "more effective ways of addressing the academic needs of academically under-prepared students, especially those from low-income and underserved backgrounds" (p. 3). Although continued research on this topic is vital, equally important is to incorporate and/or implement what we already know about ways to improve student success.

What Does Teaching Have To Do With This?

Kuh, Kinzie, and colleagues (2007) define *student success in college* as "academic achievement, engagement in educationally purposeful activities, satisfaction, acquisition of desired knowledge, skills, and competencies, persistence, and attainment of educational objectives" (p. vii). This definition contains broad and various accomplishments. As a campus community of educators, it is therefore vital that we recognize that everyone on a college campus has (or should have) a role in contributing to student success and in improving our campus climate. "Recent trends have seen retention increasingly recognized as the responsibility of all educators on campus—faculty and staff—even when there are specialized staff members solely dedicated to improving retention on campus" (Berger et al., 2012, p. 9).

Paramount to student success, Tinto (2006–2007) notes that we now have "a widely accepted notion that the actions of the faculty, especially in the classroom, are key to institutional efforts to enhance student retention" (p. 5). Yet, as colleges and universities have added programs to promote student retention and success, "regrettably, faculty involvement is still more limited than it should be" (Tinto, 2006–2007, p. 5). When it comes to content subject matter, most college professors are considered to be experts, but "simply having the expert's knowledge is not enough to be able to teach others" (Cox, 2009, p. 168). When examining the research on pedagogy methods and techniques, "expertise in a particular domain does not guarantee that one is good at helping others learn it" (Bransford, Brown, & Cocking, 2000, p. 44). If we, as professors, are to play a major role in student retention and success, then it is imperative that we, as part of our preparation for teaching, continue to explore and use teaching methods that promote student engagement and learning.

Tinto (2006–2007) suggested that "while most faculty are willing to publicly proclaim the importance of retaining each and every student, they typically do not see retaining students as their job" (p. 9). Yet, we know that effective teaching variables have a high correlation with student achievement (Feldman, 1996, 2007; Marsh & Roche, 1997) and that student achievement is closely correlated to students remaining in college and graduating. Thus, we must remain vigilant to include faculty (and faculty development programs) as we seek ways to improve student success.

Finally, it is noteworthy that "in two separate surveys on what matters the most for student success—quality of teaching and a caring faculty and staff were at the top of the list (Habley et al., 2012: 219)" (Gabriel, 2016, p. 181). I believe professors are eager to have students be engaged in their courses and have success in achieving the intended learning outcomes for their courses. This book focuses on teaching techniques, but it also includes some suggestions on how faculty and student affairs personnel can support each other when it comes to serving students.

Significance of the Teaching Professor

To improve teaching and learning at the college level, we, as professors, have numerous opportunities to investigate, expand, and analyze our pedagogy. We need to recognize that it is important to take the time to plan and prepare so that we can do our best when we are in the classroom. What happens in our classroom is not the *only* factor to consider, but it is one that has a significant impact on students' retention, persistence, and success at a college or university. The entire campus community should take on the challenge of increasing the retention, persistence, and overall success of *all* students, in particular, the students who struggle and/or are underserved.

Faculty are uniquely situated to effectuate these goals on a daily basis, because those who are teaching typically have more direct interaction with students than any other persons employed by the college or university. Yet, the role of the faculty in this mission is not always specific, especially when it comes to their teaching or instructional approaches and classroom interactions with students. In this book, which is a continuation of my previous book, I attempt to address that lack of specificity by examining additional teaching methods and techniques, especially evidence-based instructional practices, geared toward reaching all the students in our classrooms, including those who traditionally have been underrepresented and the least successful in staying in college and reaching the ultimate goal of earning a degree or certificate. And, of course, we need to reach out to our most vulnerable students "without sacrificing high standards or expectations" (Gabriel, 2008, p. 5).

While this book is not a panacea, my hope is that it will contribute to supporting your teaching methods and your efforts to improve student learning and engagement in your courses. "Take the ideas you like, and tweak the ones that don't quite fit your teaching styles, but above all, realize that you can make a difference in helping at-risk students learn how to become successful college students" (Gabriel, 2008, p. 8).

Overview of the Chapters

Chapter 2, "Class Climate," discusses many different ways we can incorporate and promote student interaction as part of our teaching practices. By setting up situations so that students can make connections and meet people from different backgrounds, we can also promote a positive classroom climate that embraces diversity. As part of our college or university culture, we can not only purposefully help our diverse students be engaged in our course material but also foster student interaction across social barriers that may exist on our campuses. By developing a "community of learners" where students can work together on the course content and do so with students from all walks of life, we can "widen" our classroom circle to include all.

Chapter 3, "The First Month of the Semester," considers classroom protocols and how our policies can impact student engagement and learning. In addition, I discuss the importance of students connecting with class content, which, in turn, will increase their learning. To accomplish this goal, I address several techniques, from activiting prior knowledge to nurturing students' commitment to the course. Having real-world issues can also help students recognize the relevancy of the course, and the value of continuing the practice of incorporating culturally relevant material is discussed as well.

Chapter 4, "Motivation and Attitudes," examines the different dispositions, attitudes, or outlooks that students may have toward their own ability to learn and how such views can impact their motivation and dedication to their studies. This chapter also discusses the research on mental toughness and what we can do to promote growth mindsets and resilience to complete one's course of study in college. As professors, we often observe students displaying behaviors that are not conducive to learning. Having ways to respond to such students can be beneficial.

Chapter 5, "Interactive Lectures," is about making our lectures more productive for student learning. This chapter also addresses the bias effect that traditional lectures can have. Still, lectures have a vital role, and for most professors they continue to be a major component of their pedagogy toolbox. Thus, having ways to improve and transform the "traditional" lectures so that our lectures stimulate and encourage active learning is essential. This chapter also discusses the use of PowerPoints and handouts, as well as the importance of students taking notes.

Chapter 6, "Reading Assignments and Class Discussions," explores aspects of choosing and using textbooks, journal articles, and other types of reading assignments. Many students struggle with reading assignments, and it often appears that they did not complete the readings, especially when they are unable to answer questions or make comments about the material. Perhaps they did read but are having comprehension or expression problems. Thus, I discuss ways to address these difficulties as well as methods for getting students to read the assigned reading and then to reflect, apply, and analyze those readings. In addition, I tackle ways to cultivate students' critical thinking skills.

Chapter 7, "Writing Assignments," discusses how we can use both low-stakes and substantive papers to help students master the learning outcomes and goals for our courses. In their research on writing, Graham and Hebert (2010) found that writing is a powerful tool for improving students' reading comprehension and critical thinking skills; however, finding a way to have students write without the grading of such assignments overwhelming us can be difficult. By using short writing exercises during class and giving corrective feedback, we can prepare our students for substantive longer assignments and research papers. I also address steps for preventing plagiarism and improving students' skills at evaluating sources.

In Chapter 8, "Resilience, Habits, and Persistence," I discuss vital concepts that can have a positive impact on student retention and can also stimulate hope and confidence for those who are facing academic struggles. As professors, we can introduce concepts of academic resilience to all of our students. We can also help students establish constructive habits and routines that will help them be successful in college and in their future careers. Additionally, I discuss the positive impact of the Productive Persistence project for struggling students. As we reach out to minority, low-income, first-generation, and academically at-risk students, we can support and encourage them to overcome obstacles as they pursue a college degree.

Conclusion

Faculty should not play a minor role in moving the needle on student retention, persistence, and graduation rates; rather, they should be major contributors. Knowing the importance of excellent teaching and the powerful influence that professors can have on students, we should strive to continually develop and improve our own teaching methods and techniques that will promote student learning, commitment, and responsibility. In short, we can boost student engagement and motivate students to be enthusiastic about their learning by using learner-centered teaching methods that can maximize the college experience.

This task is not an easy one, and there are no easy answers. "No single intervention strategy will adequately prevent all students from departing college" (Seidman, 2012, p. 77). Still, reaching out to struggling students in order to close the graduation gap among student groups without lowering standards not only is possible, but is worthy of our attention. Furthermore, I believe we have a responsibility to these students

> both as members of an institution and as individuals . . . [to] use a myriad of actions that will provide unprepared [and/or struggling] students with real opportunities for success. If we do not, we are simply setting these students up for failure and, at the same time, only pretending we have somehow fulfilled a moral obligation of providing opportunities to our diverse population in today's society. (Gabriel, 2008, p. 4)

Ultimately, we can have a positive impact on student retention and graduation rates. It takes time and commitment from us and from our students. By having a "can-do" attitude, we, as professors (no matter how long one has been teaching), can address the challenges and help close the graduation gap that exists at most of our institutions. When we do that, both individuals and society as a whole will benefit.

Notes

1. In the literature, the terms *unprepared, underprepared,* and *at risk* are used. Yet, *at risk* can also refer to a variety of problems that might be classified as social or student affairs issues (e.g., financial problems, housing issues, emotional problems). In this book, I address assisting students who are academically unprepared for college. That is, they do not have college-level academic skills when they start college.

2. Although definitions can vary somewhat throughout the literature, in this text, *retention* is defined as returning students who stay at the same institution where they initially enrolled; *persistence* is defined as students staying in higher education even if they transfer or go to more than one institution.

2

CLASS CLIMATE

Widening the Circle for a Diverse Student Body

Though it is sometimes very difficult to imagine our nation totally free of racism and sexism, my intellect, my heart, and my experience tell me that it is actually possible. For that day when neither exists, we must all struggle.

—James Baldwin (1924–1987)

Introduction

To improve retention, persistence, and success (graduation rates) of students, "the actions of faculty and staff are recognized as key variables" (Kinzie, Gonyea, Shoup, & Kuh, 2008, p. 23). When exploring students' interaction with faculty, experiences within the classroom and those outside the classroom are not usually separated but discussed as one topic. As Tinto (1997a) points out, the classroom experience itself has not been at the center of attention in retention and persistence theories even though it has a valuable and important role. He adds that time students spend in class "lies at the center of the educational activity structure of institutions of higher education; the educational encounters that occur therein are a major feature of student educational experience" (p. 599). It is that time students spend with us, their professors, beginning on the first day of class and continuing throughout the semester, that can become the most significant part of their educational experience.

As we design our courses and prepare to teach, we must keep in mind who our students are and will be. The diversity makeup of the students in our classes continues to grow. Morales (2014) notes:

> According to a recent report from National Center for Education Statistics, by the year 2022, White and Asian students will increase their attendance on college campuses by 7%, whereas the rate will be 26% for African American students and 27% for Hispanics, two groups with disproportionately higher poverty rates. (p. 92)

Additionally, more and more of our students will also be first generation, have low socioeconomic status, and be academically unprepared (Carey,

2008; Gabriel, 2008; Kelly, Schneider, & Carey, 2010). As we, the professors, focus on the classroom experience that our students will have, we must aim to create an inclusive learning community where all of our students feel welcome and have a sense of belonging. The purpose of this chapter is to provide basic building blocks (the what and how) for accomplishing these goals as well as considering "why" doing so is essential for the retention and success of our students.

Many of our nontraditional students are making adjustments not only "to a new academic environment, but also as an adjustment to a new social and cultural context" (Locks, Hurtado, Bowman, & Oseguera, 2008, p. 259). We can support our students with their adjustments by encouraging student interactions and fostering a community of learners within our classes. This means we must go beyond having a welcome message in our syllabus. From the beginning, we should explain and discuss with students different strategies that we will use to create an inclusive and positive class climate.

As professors, it is also our responsibility to increase our own cultural competence and engage in self-reflection regarding our own experiences with diversity and possible unconscious biases. This chapter includes resources to assist in this task. Finally, many of the recommendations (pedagogy, or teaching methods) suggested in this chapter, and throughout the rest of this book, represent expansions of recommendations advocated in my previous book (Gabriel, 2008). For both books, one main overall message is this: Because we have the power to create circumstances for student success in our classrooms, retention is one of our core responsibilities.

Promote a Positive Classroom Climate

As professors, we are the leaders of our courses and have the responsibility of controlling the look and feel of the classes we teach, whether they are in a physical or virtual space. Promoting a positive climate can have a powerful and constructive effect on student engagement and learning. Weimer (2016) notes that "classrooms are unique spaces—sacred in the sense that what happens in a classroom can changes lives. They're spaces dedicated to learning, where students find the motivation to learn, and where learning happens in conjunction with others and from others" (p. 1). Every semester, taking the time during the first few class periods to promote a positive classroom climate is something that we can all do, whether we are teaching upper or lower division or even graduate classes.

There are many techniques professors can use to generate a positive classroom climate. Whichever methods are chosen, we can start the process on the first day of class and continue using them throughout the semester so that a welcoming atmosphere is promoted for all our students, no matter their ethnicities, social-economic backgrounds, or educational preparedness. To set the tone early, I recommend arriving at the classroom at least 10 minutes before the class is scheduled to begin so that you can greet the students (by name if possible) as they enter the classroom. This technique also provides time where we can chat briefly with small groups of students about school or other topics. The greeting can be as simple (and obvious) as "How was your weekend?" or "How are your classes going?" Such simple conversations can lead to more in-depth conversation and personal relationships as the semester moves along. In my experience, having a personal connection to my students has increased class participation and general class enthusiasm based on a greater mutual respect between professor and students.

As we converse with our students as they enter our classrooms, we are also modeling face-to-face conversation and encouraging them to talk to each other. Experienced professors might recall that before smartphones and texting became so ubiquitous, students would visit with each other before class started. Today, however, many students enter class with their headphones on or are engrossed in their smartphones, which decreases casual person-to-person interactions. Nonetheless, professors can intervene in a very casual way. I have witnessed the following scenario many times: As I greet two or three students and start a small conversation with them, these students will take out their earphones and continue talking to each other even as I move on to greet more students who are entering the classroom. Just by starting the conversation and being friendly, students often engage with those around them and casually visit with each other. By taking this simple step before class has officially started, the atmosphere becomes welcoming and positive.

Having a positive classroom climate, in addition to the institution's welcoming climate, is of utmost importance "because of clear evidence that it affects performance, health, the extent to which potential is developed, and talent expressed" (Fleming, 2012, p. 35). Negative climates can have a negative impact on retention for all of our students (Fleming, 2012). Classrooms should also be safe and "free of physical threats and intimidation . . . [where] students wrestle with new ideas, different ways of thinking and better ways of doing tasks" (Weimer, 2016, p. 2). In addition, negative racial discrimination or gender bias should not be permitted in the classroom. (For further discussion see Fleming's research later in this chapter.)

Professors should keep in mind that some incoming students (e.g., freshmen or transfers) can be fearful of college or nervous about talking directly to their professors. This may be especially true for those who are academically unprepared for college (Gabriel, 2008). Many students admit to feeling intimidated and afraid to talk to their professors (Cox, 2009). If students attend a class where the professor appears distant and unwelcoming (even if that is not actually the case), this situation, especially for the less prepared students, can be daunting and discouraging. However, if the professor is available for casual conversation before and after class, this can ease their apprehensions about college and help them feel welcome and comfortable.

Fleming (2012) found that some professors pay less attention to minority students, ignore them, or even withhold encouragement. This kind of treatment has "been linked directly to minority-majority achievement gaps" (p. 8). However, creating a welcoming climate can help underserved students overcome their nervousness and enable them to talk to us. It is often in office hours or other times for a one-on-one meeting when we can have personal conservations with our students, and they will ask us for guidance and advice. Watson, Terrell, Wright, and Associates (2002) suggest that "as educators, we might increase the one-on-one interactions we maintain with students to understand their needs as individuals" (p. 113). These kinds of meetings can make the difference in students' understanding of the class content and assignments, so that their overall performance in the class improves and, indeed, their final grade.

In addition to greeting students as they come into the class, it is helpful to have a welcome message in the syllabus. In almost every college class, professors take the first and/or the second class to cover the course syllabus. As we review the syllabus with the students, we can elaborate on the welcome message. Having this message in writing also allows professors to reiterate it throughout the semester. For students who traditionally have low retention and graduation rates, a welcoming message can be especially meaningful. If historically underrepresented students "feel that higher education is a closed system that doesn't welcome 'outsiders' . . . anything we can do to help all of our students feel comfortable in our courses . . . goes a long way toward motivating them to succeed" (Grunert O'Brien, Millis, & Cohen, 2008, p. 45). For online courses, professors can post a written welcome message, and if possible a video welcoming the students to the course.

There are many examples available on the Internet and/or at faculty teaching or support centers. One of the best resources is the book *The Course Syllabus: A Learning-Centered Approach* by Grunert O'Brien and colleagues (2008). Some colleges have faculty development resources and templates to help teachers write a welcome message. Figure 2.1 shows opening statements from Los Angeles Southwest College (n.d.).

The welcome message can also include information regarding one's teaching philosophy. It is helpful if there is an optimistic tone and a brief reference to how the course material can be used outside of the course. Figure 2.2 shows two examples of welcome messages I have used for two different undergraduate courses.

Figure 2.1. Examples of opening statements.

(Template 1) Welcome Students:
I look forward to working with you over the next ____ weeks in [COURSE NAME]. Get ready for a journey of a lifetime. In this class you will learn about ____, ____, and ____.

(Template 2) Welcome to the Spring Semester:
Welcome to [COURSE NAME]. My name is [NAME], and I am your instructor in this course. In addition to welcoming you to the course, I would like to give you some helpful information and a few hints for successful completion of this course.

Figure 2.2. Examples of welcome messages.

Example One:
Welcome to SPED 564: Management of Learning Environments, a very special prerequisite course for several teacher preparation programs. This course will give you a foundation for learning how to set up and manage both general and special education classrooms. The overall goal is for you to learn how to create an atmosphere that is welcoming, safe, civil, inclusive, and also one that optimizes student learning. I hope you will find this course to be challenging, useful, and an enriching experience. Please call or email me if your have any questions or concerns about this class. And, welcome to the class! —*Dr. Gabriel*

Example Two:
Welcome to SPED 343: Overview of Special Education. I hope you will find this course beneficial as you are preparing to become a teacher. We live in a diverse society, and as a teacher, you will have students from all walks of life and with different abilities and disabilities. Knowing more about the different types of disabilities that some students may have can help prepare you to be a more effective teacher. We will explore ways that you can create a classroom environment that is safe, inclusive, and accepting of those with disabilities. We will also address multicultural and bilingual aspects of special education that should be very useful to you whether you decide to pursue a general or special education teaching credential . . . [message continues with information on class logistics].
—*Dr. Gabriel*

Grunert O'Brien and colleagues (2008) note that the syllabus can set the tone of our class and be used to convey our desire to create an inclusive, welcoming, and respectful atmosphere for our classroom. The "dialogue begins with the syllabus and reduces the mystery that inhibits many students' learning" (p. 26). For many minority, first-generation, low-income, and academically unprepared students, who do not have a "level of comfort" conducive for engagement and learning, we can use the welcome message in the syllabus to convey how approachable and available we are to help them with their questions and concerns. Thus, the message can be used to start class discussion, and this is also a wonderful time to let our students know about class climate goals.

Regardless of the methods a professor chooses, we should strive to welcome *all* of our students to our classes and let them know that we are looking forward to spending the semester with them. Welcoming students to our classes can be the impetus for a climate of acceptance and tolerance for students of different backgrounds.

Embrace Students' Diversity

One of Chickering and Gamson's (1987) "Seven Principles for Good Practice in Undergraduate Education" that directly addresses diversity is for professors to "respect diverse talents and ways of learning" (p. 6). When considering how to implement their advice, I believe we must go beyond respecting diverse talents. We must value and embrace diversity—not only diverse talents, but also diversity in ethnicity, socioeconomic backgrounds, and even academic readiness for college. Failing to do so can have a negative impact on students' learning, the development of their talents, and their retention and persistence. From his empirical study of two-year colleges, Opp (2002) reported that in colleges where there are "faculty and staff who do not appreciate the value of student diversity . . . [there is] a racial climate that hinders the talent development process for students of color" (p. 157). This kind of negative atmosphere impacted the overall retention and success rate for minority students.

The same kind of results have also happened at four-year colleges. According to Wathington (2005), "Many college campuses continue to be haunted by inhospitable racial climates—a fact often cited by students of color as a reason for departure . . . . Minority students' expressions of alienation, exclusion, and discrimination on predominantly white campuses remain an issue" (p. 190). When examining predominantly White colleges, Moore (2001) found overall faculty interaction with minority students to be particularly poor.

In another study, Fleming (2012) states that in classrooms where professors did not embrace and respect diversity, 71% of the students of color reported greater tensions with faculty than White students. The students of color also felt that they "were treated differently in classroom, and they were concerned about being graded unfairly" (Fleming, 2012, p. 40). A negative climate in the classroom can lead to lower numbers of student retention and persistence. Knowing this puts us, the professors, squarely in the middle of the issue of retention and persistence at our colleges, especially for underserved students.

The foregoing data illustrate that professors can be integral to retention and persistence of students in our courses by fostering an environment of inclusion. Many professors may feel that we, as individuals, do not have the power to change or influence the whole campus, especially when teaching at medium or large campuses. Although serving on university committees is a laudable goal and can effect change, that change can be difficult to measure. However, we each have the power to control what goes on in our classrooms. Thus, one by one, professors can be change agents.

Watson and colleagues (2002) remind us that our students, specifically our students of color, want to be included, "want to learn from their professors and from each other . . . want to participate and be recognized and appreciated for their participation" (p. 106). We can make sure that this happens in our classrooms. Presumably, nearly every professor already attempts to promote a classroom climate where students from all walks of life can feel welcomed and valued. The question is, are we doing so in an effective manner? Many of us can improve our classroom's climate by ensuring that we are overtly embracing the diversity of our students. Professors cannot leave it up to the campus administrators or student affairs personnel to be the only ones who promote multiculturalism activities and discussions on campus. Instead, we can directly impact our students' lives in our classrooms, which are fully within our control.

Even for those who teach at predominantly White institutions (PWIs) with few minority students in their classes, the topics of diversity and inclusion can, and should, be part of all college classes. As Heuberger, Gerber, and Anderson (1999) explain,

> Given the political, economic, social, and educational interactions that are part of our global society, people must develop cultural competence in a world that is increasingly multicultural. That competence includes knowledge of how culture influences stereotypes, perceptions, and actions, along with the ability to communicate across cultures. (p. 107)

In addition, no matter the makeup of our classrooms, we have to be conscientious of ways to ease cultural tensions that might arise in a classroom and have ways to "nurture and support minority students' educational experiences" (Watson et al., 2002, p. xii). To be prepared to do so, all professors, especially those who are not from historically underserved populations, can seek ways to increase their own cultural competence.

Increase Our Own Cultural Competence

One way that professors can increase their own cultural competence is to read both nonfiction and fiction material that addresses multicultural issues. In Appendix A, I have put together a list of fiction and nonfiction books that deal with multicultural topics and/or issues. The list includes books written by African American, Mexican American, and Native American authors and a few articles dealing specifically with ethnicity, diversity, and inclusion.

Although it is not an exhaustive list, I am sharing titles of books that I found helpful to me personally to expand my knowledge. I am considered by society's definitions as a White person, and I grew up in a small rural community with little exposure to different minority cultures and people of different ethnicities. Before I was 18 years old, my personal experience of interactions with people from different walks of life was limited. Reading expanded my horizons, in addition to my experiences and interactions in college, so I could become more culturally aware and culturally responsive in my teaching.

Furthermore, part of increasing our own cultural competence also means that we need to engage in self-reflection about our own experiences with diversity and "unpack" any unconscious bias that we may have. "Most of us do not wish to be viewed as bigots or as individuals harboring prejudice, but we simply lack the confidence and expertise to deal with issues of diversity" (Watson et al., 2002, p. xi). Attending conferences or workshops that focus on ethnic issues in the classroom and culturally responsive teaching practices can help us face our deficits and biases and increase our sensitivity and skills. For example, there are both regional and national Lilly Conferences on College and University Teaching and Learning (see www.lillyconferences.com); I also recommend The Teaching Professor Conference (see www.magnapubs.com/). For many of us, our college teaching, advising, and community experiences have enabled us to "widen the circle" of inclusion in our personal and public lives. It is important to set up classrooms so that the class climate is one that promotes inclusion and productive interaction of all of the students, especially for those who have been traditionally underrepresented and/or underserved.

If you are teaching on a campus with a teaching center for faculty where presentations or workshops on multicultural topics are offered, attending one of these can be helpful, especially if you are unable to attend a national conference. Some argue that diversity (or multicultural) training should be mandatory for all teaching faculty. Fleming (2012) discussed the high incidence of "negative or discriminatory behaviors by faculty" (p. 44). By attending conferences or workshops, in addition to reading books and articles, we can learn new ways to "provide cultural information on the heritage of all races, create a more receptive climate, and reduce ignorance for all" (Fleming, 2012, p. 44). (See chapter 3 for further discussion.)

Encourage Student Interactions

In 1975, Vincent Tinto first published his influential article on college retention. He hypothesized that student interaction and integration connect students to a university or college both academically and socially, and, subsequently, these explicit connections "influenced staying or leaving behavior" (Seidman, 2005a, p. 9). Promoting a positive classroom climate, embracing and acknowledging our students' diversity, and increasing our own cultural competence are all excellent ways we can begin to interact with our students. But, we can still do more.

Two additional effective ways to interact with students is to learn their names and have them fill out a short questionnaire about themselves and what they hope to learn from being in class. This demonstrates to the students that we are interested in them—not only as our students but also as people. Astin (1999b) reports that "frequent interaction with faculty is more strongly related to satisfaction with college than any other type of involvement or, indeed, any other student or institutional characteristic" (p. 525), and satisfaction with one's college experience is directly related to students staying there and persisting to graduation. A plethora of methods for learning students' names are available on the Internet and typically at faculty teaching or development centers. Many different types of short questionnaires and surveys are also available.

Professors can also provide opportunities for the students to meet and connect with each other. This includes helping them learn each other's names. The benefits are far-reaching—from increasing attendance to building a positive rapport and respect among all those in class. (It is also a "validation" practice, which is discussed in greater detail later in this chapter.) I believe it is well worth taking some class time early in the semester to facilitate these types of interactions (Gabriel, 2008).

When learning names (both teacher to students and students to students), many professors have a class activity, often referred to as icebreakers, where students get to "meet and greet" others. To expand the benefits of having icebreaker-type activities, first consider the tendency college students have to always sit in the same seat as the one they chose on the first day of class. Often, students will sit next to someone they have already met or who seems familiar. Therefore, when conducting an icebreaker activity, it is very beneficial to mix students up by creating random groups of three or four people so that they will meet new people.

The random selection of small groups should continue throughout the semester so that students will not only meet many different people, but also have the opportunity to have "contacts among students from different economic, social, and racial or ethnic backgrounds" (Kuh, Kinzie, Schuh, Whitt, & Associates, 2005, p. 219). These kinds of contacts may not happen unless we, the professors, manipulate the environment so that students are forced to sit in different groups throughout the semester.

An effective icebreaker activity for a smaller class (35 or fewer) is to have students interview each other in pairs, and then, when it is time for whole-class introductions, each partner introduces (or gives a short speech about) the person he or she interviewed instead of talking about one's self.

When setting up ways for students to meet others in the class, it is helpful to have at least three different variations. By mixing students, they will get an opportunity to work with the same group several times throughout the semester but not be limited to having serious conversations with only two or three people in class. Some professors require that students sit by someone new for each class and then leave it up to the students to accomplish this task. I prefer to have predetermined selected small groups, and throughout the semester, I have at least three different groupings. By using random selection techniques, I also make sure that student-athletes sit with nonathletes, fraternity and sorority members sit with non-Greek members, international students and/or out-of-state students sit with in-state students, and so on. Finally, in order not to waste any class time putting students in groups, I use nameplates (or tents) that have the students' names on the front and three different designated groups on the back (see Figure 2.3). I also have signs posted in the classroom so that students can go to a designated section and sit with their groups before the class period begins.

Because most college students are accustomed to sitting where they want to, it is important to share with them why they are being asked to sit in different places throughout the semester. I want the students to know that I am facilitating meeting people from different backgrounds, and that I think it is important to have these experiences. Fleming (2012) notes that when this does not happen "the lack of experience with each other [breeds] the lack of communication, misunderstanding, and avoidance" (p. 45). However, by working together, and by having random selection of small groups, the

Figure 2.3. Nameplates for names and group assignments and examples of different random groupings.

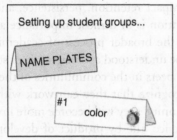
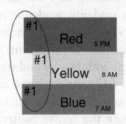

Note. The back of nameplates are used to denote three different random groups that the student will use throughout the semester.

students can increase their communication and experience with others. (Also see Appendix B: Organizing Student Interaction With Multiple Small-Group Configurations.)

As the semester progresses, the goal is for the students to have the opportunity to have "serious conversations with students of a different race or ethnicity than one's own [and]. . . serious conversations with students with different religious beliefs, political opinions, and values" (Kuh et al., 2005, p. 219). It is up to us, as educators, to allow our students to have this kind of interaction, and we can do so by using learner-centered teaching techniques in our classrooms.

Foster a Community of Learners Within Our Classes

To improve all students' first-year experience, some colleges set up learning communities, or linked courses. Learning communities have been identified as an effective practice for improving student retention and persistence for historically underrepresented populations (Kinzie et al., 2008). As Tinto (2000) states, "In their most basic form learning communities are a kind of coregistration or block scheduling that enables students to take courses together. The same students register for two or more courses, forming a sort of study team" (p. 83). However, this particular format may not be available at your institution or it may not be offered for sophomore or upper division courses. It also may not work into your teaching schedule.

Still, there is another option. As professors, we can foster a community of learners for the students enrolled in our classes. A "community of learners" is a group of people "who cooperatively engage in the exploration of ideas and knowledge" (Center for Faculty Excellence, 2009, p. 2). As we seek ways to promote our students' participation in a collaborative and cooperative way, we are also fostering them to be part of a community of learners. When considering how our classes impact retention, persistence, and success of our students, academic integration is of utmost importance and, as Tinto (1997a) notes, "by extension, the broader process of academic and social integration (involvement) can be understood as *emerging from* student involvement with faculty and student peers in the communities of the classrooms" (p. 617). As our students recognize that they can work with each other and join in the classroom community, they will become more involved with learning the course content. Hence, the by-product of developing a community of learners is improved student learning for *all* students in your classes.

Professors can also confirm and support students by using academic *validation practices* to foster a community of learners, because such practices can give students a sense of belonging, a vital component for improving retention and persistence rates. Hurtado, Alvarado, and Guillermo-Wann (2012) explain,

> Validation involves demonstrations of recognition, respect, and appreciation for students and their communities by faculty and staff, and its positive impact on persistence has been demonstrated for some less traditional student populations, including underrepresented racial/ethnic groups and community college students. (p. 4)

Rendon (2006) also points out that the concept of validation does not assume that students know how to make connections and get involved, or even know how to ask for help. In fact, Rendon found that "underserved students who have experienced invalidation in the past (e.g., being called stupid or lazy; being told 'you will never succeed in life') are not likely to get involved and/or utilize campus services easily" (p. 6). These students may also be afraid to talk to their professors, participate openly in class, or even ask questions in class for fear of looking incompetent.

As professors, we can make purposeful attempts to counter invalidation experiences by actively using validation practices in order to "assist students to 'trust their innate capacity to learn and to acquire confidence in being a college student'" (Hurtado et al., 2012, p. 5). Some validation practices have already been discussed in this chapter, such as welcoming students to class, both in person and in writing (e.g., on the syllabus). "For students who do not have time for traditional college involvements or do not have as much peer contact, it is important to note that they get their cues from faculty and staff about whether the educational environment is inclusive and welcoming" (Hurtado et al., p. 17). Welcome messages can support students who are transferring, minority students, or low-income students arriving at elite PWIs (Locks et al., 2008).

Another simple yet effective validation practice is to call students by their names. Calling students by their names not only builds rapport, increases student attendance, and promotes a sense of belonging but also "fosters student success, particularly for historically underserved students" (Kinzie et al., 2008, p. 33). Other validation practices include "praising students, providing encouragement and support, encouraging students to see themselves as capable of learning, and providing vehicles for students to support and praise each other" (Kinzie et al., 2008, p. 33).

Validation practices can motivate students to respond to our expectations and the academic rigor of our courses. They are not meant to have us lower our academic standards. As Gabriel (2008) notes, we can support our students "with teaching strategies and methods that will promote student engagement and improve performance for all the students . . . especially for those who are at-risk or unprepared, without sacrificing high standards or expectations" (p. 5). Providing positive and corrective feedback is another example of how we can hold students accountable for their academic performance and, at the same time, let them know that they are capable of meeting the high standards we have set. As I tell my students, "I would lower the standards only if I thought you couldn't do it." (See chapters 6 and 7 for further discussion on positive and corrective feedback, which is also a validation practice.)

Finally, as professors, we can use validation practices to promote a common mission for the students to achieve the course's learning goals and outcomes (or objectives) and "moderate the effects of a negative campus climate on students' sense of belonging" (Hurtado et al., 2012, p. 9). Opp (2002) notes that "peer interactions between students of color help[s] to promote a sense of belonging and commitment to the college" (p. 160). For Latino students, having a sense of belonging was especially essential for improving retention rates. Furthermore, in their extensive study, Kuh and colleagues (2005) also note a condition that promoted student success was when faculty members "recognize the value of peer interaction and facilitate such contacts" (p. 249).

An activity that I have found to be extremely useful for encouraging the development of a community of learners is one I learned from Professor Beverly Tatum, now retired, but former president of Spelman College, and author of *"Why Are All the Black Kids Sitting Together in the Cafeteria?" and Other Conversations About Race* (1997). I was fortunate to have been in the audience when Tatum had everyone participate in this exercise, and I have used it with my students ever since. At the end of the semester, most of the students list this activity as one of the most remembered and valued parts of the class—even though it is an activity that is not directly related to the course content. It is a way to learn about each other and build a community of learners in our classroom. The activity takes about 10 minutes to do—at the most 15. I believe it is well worth the time.

To set up the exercise, I tell my students that the exercise is a way to embrace the diversity of our community of learners. Tatum also recommended that we share with our students that we want them to explore who they are, where they come from, and what they bring to the table. I have encountered some who say that they do not have culture since it is so pervasive. In response, I usually tell them that just because they have not noticed their culture, it does not mean they do not have one. We all have culture, and the exercise described here can help students recognize where they are from and learn about their classmates too.

Next, so that the students can hear an example before they write their own poems, I read to them the poem I wrote about myself. After reading my poem to them, I pause and then give the directions found in Figure 2.4 so that they can write their own poems.

Figure 2.4. "I am from . . ." exercise.

TO THE STUDENTS: Your task is simply respond to the stem "I am from . . ." with the prompts I am going to give you. You will have about one minute for each.

First Stanza: Write "I am from" and list familiar items, sights, sounds, and/or smells from your home. (To the teacher: Wait one minute so students can write before going on.)

Second Stanza: Write "I am from" and list familiar foods, or dishes, especially those that you had at family gatherings. (To the teacher: Wait one minute so students can write before going on.)

Third Stanza: Write "I am from" and list familiar family sayings—those things that you heard growing up (think of your parents' voice in your ear!). (To the teacher: Wait one minute so students can write before going on.)

Last Stanza: Write "I am from" and list familiar people—family members, friends, those who link you to your past. (To the teacher: Wait one minute so students can write before going on.)

Note. Directions adapted from Professor Beverly Tatum's 1997 presentation.

Once the students have finished, I invite them to share their poems in small groups (at least three students but no more than four). After they have shared their poems and talked with each other about them, I ask if anyone would like to share his or her poem with the whole class.

There are many reasons why I think this activity is so powerful. It brings the students together in a positive way for sharing their diverse backgrounds, and it strengthens the class's sense of belonging to a "community of learners." At the same time, it allows individual recognition and promotes a feeling of respect for each other.

Many first-, second-, and even third-year college students might not be able to tell us ahead of time that being in a class where they feel they are an important part of the setting and have an opportunity to interact with classmates from different backgrounds would be an essential aspect of the college experience. However, once students encounter these types of classrooms, many are able to express how much they like being a part of such a class and how their own learning was enhanced with these kinds of interactions. We know that students prefer to be "treated as respected individuals and achieve more when instructors have a positive attitude toward both the course content and the students themselves . . . . [We can] show students from the very beginning that [we] view them as individuals within a community of learners and care about them as people" (Center for Faculty Excellence, 2009, p. 1).

Conclusion

Top researchers Tinto (2006–2007, 2012) and Astin (1999b) consider integration and involvement, respectively, to be key ingredients for increasing retention and promoting success. Our classrooms and teaching techniques can be an environment that supports (or one that does not support) our diverse students and is an environment that we control. Study after study has confirmed the impact of open and inclusive classroom environments and the enhanced learning that comes with it. This has a direct effect on students' sense of fulfillment and their persistence and retention. Thus, how we set up our classrooms and implement these techniques is of utmost importance. When seeking to help *all* of our students have a positive experience in college, we can consider ways to create an environment that will promote our students' potential and talent and at the same time demonstrate to our students that we value their diversity.

3

THE FIRST MONTH
OF THE SEMESTER

Engage, Connect, and Commit

Education is our passport to the future, for tomor-
row belongs to the people who prepare for it today.

—*Malcolm X (1925–1965)*

Introduction

As discussed in the previous chapter, we know that student engagement, or involvement, is of utmost importance for our classrooms. As Seidman (2012) puts it, "Quite simply, the more students are academically and socially involved, the more likely are they to persist and graduate . . . . Nowhere is involvement more important than in the classrooms and laboratories of the campus" (p. 257). As professors, many of us have engagement expectations in our syllabi, often referred to as course protocols or policies.

Ideally, all students would be engaged in all our classes, but we know that is not always the case. Many of us have had students who appeared to be detached, uninterested, and even disengaged, and they may not realize that this is negatively impacting their learning. However, by clarifying our in-class engagement expectations, and openly discussing how these impact their learning, students will not be left to "figure it out" on their own.

Student effort is often affected by students' perceptions of the relevancy of the class and/or course curriculum and whether or not the course material "connects" to their own interests. Thus, it is important to cultivate connections between students' prior knowledge and interests. In addition, we can increase relevancy by bringing in real-world issues that relate to our course as well as culturally relevant material. By doing this, students' motivation usually increases along with students' class involvement. It is especially important that we do this for our minority, first-generation, and academically unprepared students, because studies have shown that student engagement and effort for these students are better predictors of college success than any of their precollege characteristics (Kuh, Kinzie, et al., 2006, 2007; Laird, Chen, & Kuh, 2008; Reason, Terenzini, & Domingo, 2006).

Finally, we can promote a higher level of student learning and success by asking students to make a commitment to be engaged. When we ask students to do this, we are assisting them in fulfilling our engagement expectations.

Class Protocols (or Policies)

Tinto (2006–2007) states, "Involvement, or what is increasingly being referred to as engagement, matters, and it matters most during the critical first year of college" (p. 4). Tinto makes the point that during the students' first year of college they might be unaware of the importance of engagement and of ways to become engaged, yet it is critical that they do so at this time so that they continue successfully to their second year of college. I agree that engagement matters during the freshman year, but I also believe it is critical throughout students' college experiences and becomes even more essential as they advance in their studies.

Astin (1999b) defines *engagement* as "the amount of physical and psychological energy that the student devotes to the academic experience" (p. 518). Over 30-plus years of research, Astin has continued to find that student success and retention are directly linked to student engagement. He notes, "A particular curriculum, to achieve the effects intended, must elicit sufficient student effort and investment of energy to bring about the desired learning and development" (Astin, 1999b, p. 522). More specifically, student investment, or engagement, can refer to (but is not limited to) students attending and participating in class discussions and activities, taking class notes, making reading notes or outlines of the course texts, writing papers, and preparing for tests.

In our syllabi, we often explain course protocols, or policies, that outline expectations for the class (e.g., arriving on time, bringing the textbook and other materials to class, completing homework or readings before class, staying for the whole class, and adhering to academic honesty policies). Many of our protocol expectations are similar (despite the different subjects), but, understandably, there are also differences, such as the number of absences allowed, how late work will be handled (or whether it will even be accepted), and policies on makeup exams. These types of class protocols have often been outlined so that students know what we expect from them as they invest in their "academic experience" specifically in our class. When discussing these protocols, we can also share our rationales for them. When rationales are shared with students, most will "understand why the rules exist," which can be crucial for "student buy-in" (M. N. Thompson, 2013, p. 68).

Additionally, in a course syllabus we might refer to, or use, terms that first-generation college students may not be familiar with, and they may "fear that they are the only ones who need an explanation . . . [so they] may be hesitant to ask" (McKeachie, 2001, p. 134). For example, terms such as *plagiarism, midterm, prerequisite, drop before census, appropriate documentation, academic integrity,* and *peer-reviewed journals* may be confusing, and we can be supportive, especially for first-year students, by going over these terms as we discuss the syllabus with our students.

Many of our students do not know how we, their professors, characterize the actions and/or behaviors that they demonstrate in class as indicators of their engagement in our courses. Some students are totally unaware of the fact that certain behaviors signal negative attitudes or signs of disengagement (e.g., reading a newspaper, texting on a phone, surfing on a computer, side-chatting with a neighbor, sleeping). However, we can be proactive to prevent misunderstandings by clarifying and discussing our in-class engagement expectations.

In-Class Engagement Expectations

If we want our students to be engaged, then we must lead by example. We cannot simply be "stand-and-deliver" lecture-type professors whose students sit passively listening and taking notes. We must heed the advice given in Chickering and Gamson's (1987) *Seven Principles for Good Practice in Undergraduate Education.* One of the seven principles is for professors to encourage active learning. The authors elaborate, "Learning is not a spectator sport . . . . [Students] must talk about what they are learning, write about it, relate it to past experiences and apply it to their daily lives. They must make what they learn part of themselves" (Chickering & Gamson, 1987, p. 4). However, for our classrooms, inspiring the engagement behaviors is contingent on us, the professors, through the use of active learning techniques and methods.

How students are to interact with us and with each other in class is not usually discussed, in part because we expect students to already know how to be respectful and attentive. However, because professors often see behaviors that they consider disrespectful and/or disengaging, it is helpful to clarify the kind of engagement expectations we have for our classes. Following is an excerpt of a statement that I use on a syllabus for an undergraduate class where I clarify my expectations:

The course will be taught using learner-centered teaching methods. During small and large group activities, I expect you to interact with your classmates by talking, listening, sharing, brainstorming, problem solving, etc . . . . Thus, all students are asked to keep their cell phones put away, and laptops or iPads will not be used during class presentations or class discussions. (Using technology during class—iPod, texting, cell phone, or computer—inappropriately will affect your class activity points/grade.) Remember, you have the right to express your views and the right to be listened to, as do your classmates. Thus, it is important that we all listen and talk to each other, and not be distracted by our phones or text messages. Being present and focused for class are ways for us to show each other our respect and appreciation for what each of us brings to the table! (We will be voting on the "Ground Rules for Class Discussions" and other activities next class.)

Another example that professors can use for describing classroom engagement expectations comes from Julie Figueroa, professor at California State University (CSU), Sacramento. She puts in her syllabus an example of a "letter of recommendation" and shares with her students that the attributes listed in a letter of recommendation should also be the traits and behaviors professors would like to see in their students (presentation at CSU, Chico, September, 2016).

A letter of recommendation written by a professor is often based on how the student performed and acted in class, so by reading excerpts of a sample letter, students can connect what they are doing in the classroom directly to a future career or employment. Arriving on time and staying for the whole class are behavioral characteristics that a professor might include in a letter of recommendation because "college attendance shapes social skills and personal habits important for adult living" (Braxton, 2006, p. 5). Professors might also comment on whether a student is prepared and attentive, makes positive contributions in class, and is respectful to classmates. "The development of such skills and habits [also] supplies [professors] with a set of indicators of college student success" (Braxton, 2006, p. 5). They are also the kinds of characteristics that future employers are looking for.

Class discussions can be formatted in different ways; for example, you might have a class discussion with the entire class (large group) or you might have discussions in which students form small groups of three or four people per group. For both types of settings, establishing ground rules can outline the expected behavioral norms so that respectful dialogues are ensured. These kinds of ground rules can be very useful as students from different ethnic and socioeconomic backgrounds learn how to communicate with each other and find commonalities. By observing them, we can help promote each of our classrooms to be a "community of learners" (see chapter 2 for further discussion).

Following is an example of ground rules for discussion by Gorski (2015):

1. Listen actively—respect others when they are talking.
2. Speak from your own experience instead of generalizing ("I" instead of "they," "we," and "you").
3. Do not be afraid to respectfully challenge one another by asking questions, but refrain from personal attacks—focus on ideas.
4. Participate to the fullest of your ability—community growth depends on the inclusion of every individual voice.
5. Instead of invalidating somebody else's story with your own spin on her or his experience, share your own story and experience.
6. The goal is not to agree—it is to gain a deeper understanding.
7. Be conscious of body language and nonverbal responses—they can be as disrespectful as words.

To introduce these discussion ground rules, I hand out a separate hard copy of Gorski's rules to the class members and have students in small groups (three to four students in a group) talk about the list for about three to four minutes. I then call on individuals from the different small groups to report their opinions on which ones they liked the best and which ones they did not like and why. The entire class then discusses the ground rules for three to four minutes, and we vote on whether or not to adopt them for our class discussions. Since I started using these ground rules, the student vote for every class I have taught has always been a unanimous "yes."

Even though students may agree to the ground rules, we, the professors, still have to make sure that the rules are upheld throughout the semester. It is a good idea to revisit and review the ground rules periodically with the students. There may even be times when we have to intervene and remind students to adhere to the ground rules. It is important to consistently set and enforce the ground rules from the beginning of the semester. Professors may find it helpful to remind the students of the purpose of the discussion ground rules, which is to ensure respectful conversation and participation by all so that all students feel welcome in our classrooms. McKeachie (2001) points out that as professors we must be sure that all of our students feel included and comfortable with us and with other class members. He gives professors and instructors the following advice:

> Welcoming involves . . . helping all students to display welcoming behavior toward one another in the classroom. We play a critical role in monitoring classroom behavior and addressing problems as part of the learning

experience when they occur. Rather than hurriedly passing over [an inappropriate stereotyping or even racist] comment of a student . . . it is important for us to openly discuss issues surrounding the negative image and language choice of the response, even if embarrassment is a possibility . . . . Teaching for diversity is not only being more welcoming to diverse groups, but also increasing the sensitivity of majority students to cultural differences. (McKeachie, 2001, p. 124)

For the students of historically underrepresented and underserved groups, we can make a difference by ensuring that all of our students are acknowledged, respected, and valued.

Importance of Making Connections

Tinto (1997a) notes that when students are engaged, involved, and connected, they put forth higher levels of effort and learn more material. However, sometimes students arrive in our classrooms without much motivation to be engaged and/or with an attitude of just getting through the class. So, while each of us wants our students to make connections to our course material, it can be challenging. Some students do not seem to have any personal interest in, awareness of, or enthusiasm for the course content. Light (2001) found that many freshmen who ended up in academic trouble were often in all general education-type classes (which were also large classes), chosen with the idea of getting the required classes "'out of the way'; these freshmen did not try to find any class that might spark an interest, engage, or 'excite them'" (p. 39). Even after students' freshman year, students need to carefully explore their class options, because they can still end up in classes they are not interested in.

Unfortunately, some older students can also have a passive, lackadaisical, and/or indifferent attitude toward some of their courses. Graunke and Woosley (2005) found that "sophomores were less likely than students in other classes to be actively involved with their own learning or to see faculty as actively engaged in their personal and academic development" (p. 370). This was especially true for students who had not found a major or were unsure whether they had selected the "correct" major for a future career. As professors, we can be especially cognizant of this situation and help students recognize (and reflect on) the relevancy of the content of the courses we are teaching.

Neumann and Neumann (1989) also noted that significant predictors of persistence for juniors and seniors came from their educational experiences and their involvement in learning activities rather than their social experiences. They refer to the educational experience as the quality of learning experience. "The three learning characteristics that are the key to maximizing students' probabilities of successfully completing their programs are student-faculty contact and students' involvement in their academic program, and the quality of course content and instructional activities" (p. 139).

Students' view on the relevancy and value of course material, the assignments, is impacted by their ability to make connections to us (their professors) and the course content. We should have active learning methods that will engage our students during our class meetings. "Students who experience active learning in their courses perceive themselves as gaining knowledge and understanding from their courses and view their course work as personally rewarding" (Braxton, Jones, Hirschy, & Hartley, 2008, p. 74). These perceptions can increase student motivation, and higher levels of motivation for both lower and upper division students can influence "how much time and energy the student devotes to the learning process" (Astin, 1999b, p. 522).

Over and over, we find that engagement and individual effort are the critical components for retention, persistence, and eventual college graduation (Pascarella & Terenzini, 2005). Moreover, as noted by Gabriel (2008, 2016), students who arrive at college unprepared for the academic rigors of college can overcome deficiencies (low academic skills) and become successful in college, but not without significant personal exertion and engagement in their courses. We can help our students with putting forth the significant effort when we help them develop connections to our course content material and its relevancy.

Activating Prior Knowledge

Activating prior knowledge refers to having students discuss and reflect on knowledge and experiences that they think they already have about the course material or subject matter. It can include information or knowledge that specifically relates to the new material, or "things that are similar to . . ." or even "this sounds like . . ." types of information. A prior-knowledge activity is very effective for connecting students' interests to the course content, and by having such an activity, professors are "sending a message to students that [we] . . . respect the knowledge they bring to the learning setting" (Grunert O'Brien et al., 2008, p. 26). In addition, when students think about what they already know about a topic, it "can help students integrate new information" (Ambrose, Bridges, DiPietro, Lovett, & Norman, 2010, p. 15).

Activating prior knowledge can be as simple as asking students to think about what they already know about a topic or specific problem and how it might be related to the new information. A type of prior-knowledge activity that I have used with much success involves students working together in small groups. The focus is on stimulating students' memory and discussing what they recall. To conduct this activity, set up your classroom by placing enough large self-stick posters (from poster pads measuring 20 inches by 23 inches) around the room to have small groups of three to five students at each poster. Have at least two large pen markers for students to write with at each poster. At the top of each poster, write a topic. You can use topics that will be covered over the course of the semester, or just topics for the first part of the semester or for the first midterm. You can have the same topic for all the posters or different subtopics on each poster. The topics should be short—similar to subtitles in a textbook.

Direct the students to work in small groups (randomly selected) and brainstorm their collective "prior knowledge," that is, what each group thinks they already know about the topic, or even information that they think will be related to the topic. Ask students to write short phrases or bullet points on the posters. (Remind students to write in large lettering so classmates can see it from their desks.) Give students at least three to four minutes to complete this task. (This part works best if it is not too long—no more than six or seven minutes.)

Next, call on one student per group to share, or have a Gallery Walk. A Gallery Walk is where the groups move around the room and read what other groups wrote. Time spent for each poster is limited or timed; for example, everyone moves clockwise to the next poster and they have 2 minutes (or less) to look at what that group wrote and respond. Blow a whistle (or ring a bell) to signal that it is time for the groups to move to the next poster. Repeat until the class has seen all the posters and students are now back at their own poster. For a large class (over 50 students), change up the reporting or simply have a silent Gallery Walk for about 5 minutes, knowing that everyone will not be able to see every poster.

This activity is based on a teaching professor conference presentation given by Ed Nuhfer, director of educational effectiveness (retired) at Humboldt State University. It can take as little as 12 minutes, and up to 20 to 25 minutes, depending on the size of the class. It is designed to help students make connections between what they have previously learned or experienced (their prior knowledge) and the current content they will be learning about in a class, and it is a way for us to demonstrate our recognition and appreciation of what our students bring to the class. "Valuing students' prior knowledge is a bridge to connecting students to the curriculum and to helping them make meaning of their educational experience" (Kuh et al., 2005, p. 205).

When we include prior knowledge in our courses, it is a way for us to send a strong message to students that we want them to "use what they have learned" (Bransford, Brown, & Cocking, 2000, p. 73). We need to consider our students' prior knowledge and their experience, especially when considering views from "different cultural backgrounds as strengths to be built on, rather than as signs of 'deficits'" (Bransford et al., 2000, p. 73), so any type of prior-knowledge survey should not be graded.

Furthermore, prior-knowledge activities can alert professors to students who are "novice" learners in the field they are teaching and then they can make plans for supporting them. Even if students reveal that their current "knowledge" is incorrect or going in the wrong direction, this is valuable information for the professor, because misconceptions or inaccurate information should be discussed, explained, and redirected. Angelo and Cross (1993) have a "Misconception-Preconception Check" activity where the "focus is on uncovering prior knowledge or beliefs that may hinder or block further learning" (p. 132). For example, students may have misconceptions or incorrect beliefs regarding the topic, and these misunderstandings can prevent them from grasping the new material. Thus, it is helpful that we know about these misconceptions and address them. Angelo and Cross note that this activity is useful for disciplines "where college students have knowledge, beliefs, and attitudes about the phenomena they will study" (p. 133).

For a prior-knowledge activity that is completed individually by each student, professors can use the "Background Knowledge Probes" by Angelo and Cross (1993). Professors prepare "short, simple questionnaires [that] . . . required [sic] students to write short answers, to circle the correct responses to multiple-choice questions, or both . . . that will probe the students' existing knowledge of [the] concept, subject, or topic" (pp. 121–123).

Above all, we must remember that "when faculty honor and celebrate student backgrounds and encourage students to make use of their prior knowledge, they empower students as learners" (Kuh et al., 2005, p. 205). Beyond the recognition and acceptance of the diverse backgrounds of our students, we are also applying a basic principle from the science of learning: "When students can connect what they are learning to accurate and relevant prior knowledge, they learn and retain more. In essence, new knowledge 'sticks' better when it has prior knowledge to stick to" (Ambrose et al., 2010, p. 15).[1]

Increase Relevancy With Real-World Issues

Introducing global perspectives that connect to your subject and field can add relevancy to your class and spark student interest for those who might not start off the semester with the kind of enthusiasm we would like our students to have. Local issues and personal experiences can promote a "connectedness" between course content and student motivation. Engstrom (2008) recognizes that student engagement increases when course content was connected "to the lives of faculty or students. Students learned when they thought the curriculum was relevant to real-life issues" (p. 11).

For all of our students, including those who are minority, first generation, and/or academically unprepared, incorporating real-world problems, events, or issues that relate to the course can be especially beneficial. Kuh and colleagues (2006) report that African American students "benefit from more occasions to make connections between the reality of their lives and learning experiences in the classroom. Students need safe spaces to express their personal views, struggle with understanding human differences, and explore their identities" (p. 72).

Sometimes being able to do this may be necessary even if you teach a subject such as math or physics that may not seem directly related to current events. Recently, across the United States, news events or protests such as those concerning police conflicts with minorities have stirred further protests and demonstrations in our cities and even on college campuses. With these types of hot issues going on in our society, we may need to take some class time to address concerns "because of inter-student dynamics" that surface in our classrooms (Warren, 2002–2006, p. 3). It is a way for us to let our students know that we care about them and about social justice in our society. The goal is not to solve the problem or make students choose sides, but rather to acknowledge the complexities of our society and assist students in achieving a level of comfort with their classmates so that conversations can expand to a deeper level. "Parker Palmer keeps reminding us, that good teaching comes from carefully woven connections 'between my students, my subject and myself.' Learning is always embedded in specific contexts and relationships" (Frederick, 1995, p. 85).

Culturally Relevant Material

Another way to increase motivation and relevancy to our courses is to incorporate interesting historical events, or significant public figures or private individuals from different ethnic groups, and items from popular media such as music, dance, literature, and film.[2] Consider the powerful movie *Stand and Deliver*, which was based on a true story and took place in a low-income, low-performing Title I high school in Los Angeles, California. The new math teacher, Jaime Escalante, tells his students, who are mostly Hispanic/Latino, "Did you know that neither the Greeks nor the Romans were capable of using the concept of zero? It was your ancestors, the Mayans, who first con-templated the zero. The absence of value. True story. You 'burros' have math in your blood" (Menendez, 1997; www.quotes.net/mquote/90269). The rest of the movie tells the story of the successful impact that Escalante had on his students as they outperformed all expectations on a rigorous advanced col-lege placement exam for calculus. Why share this story? It demonstrates how Escalante not only brought to his students a bit of proud history by referring to the Mayans, the ancestors of many of the students in his class, but also let his students know that he believed in their ability to do well in math. We can follow this great teacher's example by enriching our course content to include references and/or examples that draw on a global or world perspec-tive—not just one that comes from a Eurocentric perspective or straight out of a textbook.

When we cultivate meaningful connections to different ethnic groups, we are also addressing the issues of cultural alienation or ethnic distance between some professors and their students, or between students of different ethnic backgrounds. "Alienation also occurs frequently when students look in vain for a mention of their social group and evidence of their perspective throughout the curriculum" (McKeachie, 2001, p. 135). We can share with our class information on historical events or "role models of scholars, practi-tioners, and artists" (McKeachie, 2001, p. 134) from different ethnic groups in our fields of study or subject areas. Having examples of people from mul-tiple cultural backgrounds can be a powerful tool for building connections for all of our students—not just for historically underserved and underrepre-sented students. As professors, we must take steps to integrate diversity and multicultural topics into our classrooms in order to provide our students with a global view of a diverse world, which is a necessary perspective for success in the twenty-first century (Heuberger, Gerber, & Anderson, 1999).

Using culturally relevant instructional material is a critical element in increasing connections between our course content and our students. A study by Fleming (2012) provides an excellent example of how we can incorporate relevant cultural material into our own courses. This particular study involved academically unprepared African American students taking a college algebra class. Fleming explains that math, like much of science, is usually consid-ered a universal subject that is culturally neutral and "color blind." However, Fleming notes that culturally relevant instruction could be included in math word problems by incorporating "references to African American scenarios, issues, and history" (p. 237). The study examined the students' performances on pre-tests, exercises, and post-tests, and Fleming found that "the inclusion of culturally relevant tests and exercises contributed to better performance in college algebra, and specifically to passing the course" (p. 243).

In addition to using culturally relevant material in math, it was also demonstrated in an earlier study that "multicultural content facilitates the reading performance of at-risk college students" (Fleming, 2012, p. 235). Although professors may be concerned that incorporating content revisions to include culturally relevant material would be a very time-consuming and difficult task, Fleming (2012) noted that

> the facilitating effects of culturally relevant mathematics materials appear promising. However, what is remarkable in this effort is how little cultural relevance was required to produce significant effects on performance. Sometimes only the words *African American* in a word problem, a fleeting reference to the civil rights movements, the mere mention of 'black' business, or the implied ethnic reference by naming a historically black college was sufficient to affect performance. (p. 243)

As professors in many fields of study, who teach students from many different ethnic groups, we can find ways to start infusing culturally relevant materials into our courses. Because we are role models and mentors to our students, it is important that we take the time and effort to ensure that our classrooms, and our course materials, are culturally inclusive.

Significance of a Commitment

Eliciting student effort and energy does not come from the curriculum alone. It must be inspired by enthusiastic and engaged professors, and, of course, from the students themselves. Asking our students to do their best and to make a commitment to a class no matter how difficult the tasks appear to be is what Bain (2004) identifies as an action that the "best" college teachers do. He states, "Exceptional teachers ask their students for a commitment to the class and the learning" (p. 112). Having students verbally pledge or raise their hand to publicly declare their commitment is a way to help students "promise" to do their best. Bain further explains, "Some people [teachers] do so in the first-day exercises that lay out the promises and plans of the course. They ask students to decide if they really want to pursue the learning objectives in the manner described. Others spell out specific obligations they see as part of the decision to join the class" (p. 113). Several teachers cited in Bain's study added that once students declare that they will make a commitment to their class they will tell the students, "You have responsibilities to everyone else in this community of learners" (p. 113). These responsibilities might include coming to every class on time and staying for the entire class, bringing textbook(s) and note-taking supplies, and working cooperatively in small groups.

This student commitment is vital for making the most of our class time. It is especially important for students who commute to college. Most community colleges are in fact serving students who commute. For commuters, the classroom is their main, and often their only, contact with the college. If they are going to be involved, it is most likely to occur in the classroom. "Indeed, for students who commute to college, especially those who have multiple obligations outside the college, the classroom may be the only place where students and faculty meet, where education in the formal sense is experienced" (Tinto, 1997a, p. 599). It is during class time that we have the opportunity to interact with our students and to connect with them. (See chapter 5 for further discussion.) Attending class regularly not only promotes engagement and higher grades but also helps improve retention and success of the students (Gabriel, 1991, 2008). Asking students to make a commitment to be engaged will help students fulfill our engagement expectations.

Conclusion

The first month (and even the first week) of the semester is a critical time where professors can establish classroom engagement practices by setting up and enforcing classroom protocols and uphold the agreed-upon ground rules for different classroom activities. As we plan and design our courses to maximize student learning for all, we must also plan for ways to cultivate connections to foster an inclusive environment and demonstrate sensitivity for minority, first-generation, low-income, and academically unprepared students.

Student engagement is directly related to learning, and the learning that happens in our courses is related to student retention, persistence, and success. "Research shows that the more actively engaged students are—with college faculty and staff, with other students, and with the subject matter they study—the more likely they are to learn, to stick with their studies, and to attain their academic goals" (Bueschel, 2008, p. 4). Beginning the semester with clear expectations for engagement and solid ground rules for class discussions and finding ways to increase connections between the course material and our students are positive steps for ensuring and increasing student engagement and involvement. Taking these steps will, in turn, increase retention, persistence, and eventually graduation rates.

Notes

1. For further examples and assistance on activating prior knowledge, see https://www.cte.cornell.edu/teaching-ideas/assessing-student-learning/what-do -students-already-know.html or https://facultyinnovate.utexas.edu/learning/hlw/ prior-knowledge

2. Biographies on people from different ethnic groups who are notable in almost every field of study—science, social science, humanities, and so on—can be found on the Internet. Also see Appendix A: Readings for Expanding Cultural Competence.

4

MOTIVATION AND ATTITUDES

Impact of Mindsets and Mental Toughness Attributes

You can pray until you faint, but unless you get up and try to do something, God is not going to put it in your lap.

—Fannie Lou Hamer (1917–1977)

Introduction

As director of an academic support program that was specifically designed for academically unprepared students, I would begin every semester by discussing engaging behaviors with the students and providing a list of helpful hints for "making it" in college. Attending all classes and sitting in the front (or near the front) of the class are two behaviors that were always listed as a priority for being engaged and involved in one's classes. However, when I would go to visit classes that my students were enrolled in, I often found them in the back of the room—if not in the last row.

After visiting one class where two of my students, Mike and Denzel (not their real names), were sitting near the back of the large class, I asked them, "Why?" Why were they not sitting in the front of the room, where they could see and hear the professor? After a long moment of silence and each staring at his feet, Mike finally responded, "We *can't* sit down in front." I was stunned by the emotion in his voice, and by Denzel's agreement. I asked both of them, "Why not?" Denzel answered, "Because that's where all the smart people sit."

After we talked more, I realized that these students, as well as other at-risk students with whom I worked, felt inadequate and ill equipped to deal with the academic demands of college. Many of my students had trouble making "connections" with their professors or the subject matter being taught. If the professor did not reach out to them, they were not assertive enough, or had insufficient self-efficacy, to overcome their own uncertainty about how to become engaged in their classes. Many who started the semester with high hopes and determination to succeed started giving up and were becoming disillusioned when the first grades for midterms or papers were returned. By this time, it was usually too late to drop any class in which they were performing poorly.

Grunder and Hellmich (1996) point out that unprepared students have the most difficulty when it comes to meeting the academic challenges of college and adjusting to college life, and these students are more likely not to make it past the first year of college. Seymour (2000) indicates that the main difference between leavers and stayers (in the sciences and engineering) was "whether [students] . . . were able to surmount [their problems] . . . quickly enough to survive" (p. 82). Problems typically include things such as a lack of self-confidence, the belief that they could not be successful, loss of interest, intimidation from professors or fellow students, and even a feeling of not being accepted. While these attributes can be significant predictors for the lack of students' success, so can a person's background or academic preparation (Veenstra, 2009, p. 19). Lack of effort or low motivation is often cited as one of the main factors for a student's academic failures or a forced dismissal (for low grades).

Bligh (2000) states, "There is little doubt that student motivation is an important factor affecting the performance of students in their courses" (p. 57). In addition to being motivated, students need to know how to complete assignments and prepare for exams. However, some believe that "performance failures are frequently the result of a lack of confidence in implementing skills and strategies, not a lack of knowledge about the existence of these skills and strategies" (Klassen, Krawchuk, & Rajani, 2008, p. 928). For many students like Mike and Denzel, their confidence and willingness to engage were linked to their perceptions about intelligence along with low self-efficacy. Like these two, many at-risk students even doubt that they are "smart enough" for college.

Fortunately, the situation with Mike and Denzel was saveable—as are similar situations for many historically underrepresented students. Mindsets and mental toughness are two models that can help us, the professors, find effective ways to support our students, especially those who are struggling. Without sacrificing course content, we can introduce these two models to our students and implement interventions, which can foster students' perseverance, resilience, determination, and motivation.

Mindsets: Fixed or Growth

Dweck and Leggett (1988) found that the general perceptions students hold about intelligence influence the type of goals they have in school, and, in turn, these goals influence student motivation and the behavior students display when completing academic tasks (Dweck, 2006; Dweck & Leggett, 1988; Grant & Dweck, 2003). The two general perceptions about intelligence are defined as a *fixed mindset* or as a *growth mindset.*

Briefly, fixed mindsets are when people believe that intelligence is a "fixed entity" (Dweck, 2006, p. 6) and reflects what one has been born with, or had since birth. In other words, with a fixed mindset, the perception is that people "have a pre-determined capacity for learning—the 'container' may be large, but it is limited, and the best one can do is fill it to capacity" (Dweck & Leggett, 1988, p. 257). Students with fixed mindsets usually have performance goals (described in more detail later in this chapter).

Growth mindsets are when people believe that intelligence is an incremental or "malleable" quality, and one's intelligence can grow. With this point of view, "the capacity for learning can be extended and the container can be stretched in various directions" (Dweck & Leggett, 1988, pp. 256–257). That is, one can learn how to learn and become smarter over time. Students with growth mindsets usually adopt challenging learning goals (Dweck, 2006).

The two types of goals, performance and learning, represent significantly different points of view, and in the academic area, different types of behaviors. Students who believe intelligence is a fixed entity with performance goals "are concerned with gaining favorable judgments of their competence" (Dweck & Leggett, 1988, p. 256). Students with performance goals are also vulnerable to failure because they tend to display behaviors that can be described as a "helpless pattern . . . . [They are] characterized by an avoidance of challenge and a deterioration of performance in the face of obstacles" (Dweck & Leggett, 1988, p. 256).

I witnessed these types of behaviors and attitudes from students who believed that intelligence is fixed. Regarding the situation with Mike and Denzel (discussed at the beginning of the chapter), not only were they ready to give up as they faced difficult tasks, but they also started displaying avoidance behaviors such as missing classes, failing to engage when they were in class, and not seeking help. As Dweck (2006) notes, having a fixed mindset with performance goals will lead to these types of maladaptive behaviors.

In contrast, individuals who believe that intelligence is able to grow or that it is malleable usually have learning goals and "are concerned with increasing their competence" (Dweck & Leggett, 1988, p. 256). Students with learning goals tend to cultivate a "mastery-oriented pattern . . . [that] involves the seeking of challenging tasks and the maintenance of effective striving under failure" (Dweck & Leggett, 1998, p. 256). This can be seen when these students persist in attending class, seek out tutoring, or meet with their professors or advisers for assistance, especially when they face new and difficult tasks. Student engagement is related positively to the incremental theory because the students' beliefs about being able to increase their capacity for learning impact their engagement (Dweck, 2006; Dweck & Leggett, 1988; Dweck, Walton, & Cohen, 2014).

It is interesting to note that people can have both fixed and growth mindsets—a fixed mindset about some subjects (e.g., "I can't do math so why bother") and a growth mindset toward others (e.g., "My writing has been improving since I began working with a tutor"). Furthermore, people's mindsets can change, even when they are older (Dweck, 2006; Dweck & Leggett, 1988).

When considering student retention (as noted in previous chapters), a key ingredient is academic integration (Astin, 1999a; Bean & Eaton, 2000; Tinto, 2006–2007). However, Bean and Eaton (2000) found that "academic avoidance behaviors, such as avoiding courses or avoiding studying, had a negative relationship with academic integration. Academic approach behaviors, such as asking questions in class or pursuing tutoring, were positively related to academic integration" (p. 52). Many struggling students who are demonstrating avoidance behaviors can turn things around if they learn about growth mindsets and realize that they can improve their own brainpower. With a positive attitude toward their own potential, students tend to put in hard work. With dedication and use of learning strategies, learning can be enhanced, and students can stay involved and integrated in their courses.

Promoting Growth Mindsets

There are many ways that professors can incorporate techniques to reinforce growth mindsets that will fit in with their course content, promote student ownership of their own learning, and increase student engagement. The suggestions in this section are not exhaustive but are meant to provide a starting point for encouraging our students to have growth mindsets and learning goals. Encouraging and promoting growth mindsets can be crucial for students who are the most at risk for failing our classes and/or dropping out of school. It is important to remember that when faculty intervened and met with students who were at a crisis point in their academic or even personal life, many of those students were able to turn things around, persevere, and complete their studies as a result of these strategies (Seymour, 2000; Seymour & Hewitt, 1997). In fact, "few college experiences are more strongly linked to student learning and persistence than students' interactions with faculty members . . . . Such contacts influence changes in the cognitive, psychosocial, and attitudinal domains of students' lives" (Reason et al., 2006, p. 151). Thus, such interactions and contacts with faculty also influence students' persistence and degree completion.

Among the first things professors can do is introduce students to the mindset concepts and give them the definition of the mindset types along with the descriptions of the two different kinds of goals. Beattie (2015) recommends having your students read a short article about how intelligence can grow titled "You Can Grow Your Brain: New Research Shows the Brain Can Be Developed Like a Muscle," by Blackwell (2002).[1] In this article, the author presents a short summary on the research of how our brains change as we learn new things. Blackwell writes, "The more that you challenge your mind to learn, the more your brain cells grow . . . . By practicing, you make your brain stronger. You also learn skills that let you use your brain in a smarter way" (p. 1). Students can ponder what that means to them personally, and professors can have a class discussion or ask students to write reflections after reading the article. Beattie studied students in remedial math classes at community colleges and found that in only one month students made tremendous improvements in their exam grades. (See chapter 8 for further discussion, and see www.perts.net for the entire project.)

Another step we can take is to expose students to successful individuals who initially faced obstacles and failures and share real-world examples of growth mindsets. When students read about notable individuals who were portrayed as having inborn traits, they were more likely to lean toward a fixed mindset belief and adopt performance goals (Dweck & Leggett, 1988). However, when students were given readings about people who had to struggle, overcome obstacles, and work hard to acquire qualities to become successful, the students were more likely to adopt a growth mindset and learning goals. Assigning such readings may not fit into a professor's class, and certainly did not fit neatly into my courses, but I nonetheless wanted to expose my students to notable individuals who had worked hard to accomplish success. To do this, without taking up much class time (about three minutes a week), I present a "Quote of the Week" at the beginning of the first class each week of the semester on a PowerPoint slide that also includes the person's picture. In addition, I post the quote on our course web page (Blackboard Learn). When introducing the Quote of the Week, I briefly share with the students the hardships, obstacles, or challenges that the person had to overcome in order to become successful. The quotes are from a very diverse group of people, and from all walks of life. Some of the authors are famous, and some not so famous.

One example (see Figure 4.1), from Madam C. J. Walker (n.d.), is, "I had to make my own living and my own opportunity . . . . Don't sit down and wait for the opportunities to come. Get up and make them." Following is a brief story about her that I share with my class:

> Walker (born 1867 and died 1919) was the daughter of "emancipated" slaves, grew up extremely poor, and was not able to go to school. She married when she was only 14 years old to escape her harsh environment, but her husband died 2 years later. Walker never gave up and always worked hard (did laundry, cleaned houses, any job she could get). She was able to overcome many obstacles in order to get a basic education. Then, she invented a "hair" product, which she promoted to neighbors and friends. As it became more and more popular, she formed her own company and became a very successful businesswoman. She was one of the first American women millionaires, and still ranks among the greatest African American philanthropists in the nation's history. (Adapted from https://www.biography.com/people/madam-cj-walker-9522174)

Another example (see Figure 4.1) is James Baldwin (1924–1987). I chose this author because I first became acquainted with his works when I was in college and read his book *Go Tell It on the Mountain* (1995), first published in 1952, and reprinted several times since. Eli (1996) included words from Baldwin in his book, *African-American Wisdom: A Book of Quotations and Proverbs*: "Though it is sometimes very difficult to imagine our nation totally free of racism and sexism, my intellect, my heart, and my experience tell me that it is actually possible. For that day when neither exists, we must all struggle" (p. 90). Following is the brief story I tell my classes about Baldwin:

> James Baldwin grew up in poverty and had a harsh childhood. By the time he was 14, he was looking for a way to escape his circumstances and would spend time in libraries. There he found his passion for writing, but first he worked as a preacher, then on the "railroad" and, finally, did freelance writing. His first book was published in 1953 when he was 29 years old. It was an autobiography about his struggles growing up in Harlem, New York. "The passion and depth with which he described the struggles of black Americans were unlike anything that had been written. Though not instantly recognized as such, *Go Tell It on the Mountain* has long been considered an American classic" (www.pbs.org/wnet/americanmasters). James Baldwin wrote many other books, but it was his hard work, passion, and dedication that led to his success. By 1962, he was working full-time to help promote racial justice for all in America. His book *The Fire Next Time* demonstrates his deep involvement in the Civil Rights Movement, and his fight for human rights and dignity. (Adapted from https://www.biography .com/people/james-baldwin-9196635)

Figure 4.1. Inspiring Quote of the Week signs.

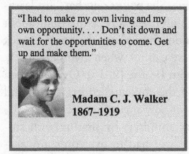

"I had to make my own living and my own opportunity. . . . Don't sit down and wait for the opportunities to come. Get up and make them."

Madam C. J. Walker
1867–1919

James Baldwin
(1924–1987)

". . . though it is sometimes very difficult to imagine our nation totally free of racism and sexism, my intellect, my heart, and my experience tell me that it is actually possible. For that day when neither exists, we must all struggle."

Note. Two examples of the "Quote of the Week" messages, put on a PowerPoint slide and also posted on the class website (Blackboard Learn). (See Appendix C for additional examples.)

How we give verbal and written feedback to students is another way to reinforce and/or promote growth mindsets. Beattie (2015), director of the Productive Persistence project at the Carnegie Foundation for the Advancement of Teaching, conducted workshops with professors and instructors on how to set up classroom cultures that promoted growth mindsets. The goal was to have professors emphasize the process of learning, which included "sustained effort, good strategies, seeking help" and deemphasized ability or already being smart in the subject matter (Beattie, 2015). The researchers involved with the Productive Persistence project worked with the professors and instructors on ways to respond to the students during different situations so that the feedback would promote growth mindsets rather than fixed mindsets. In workshops with faculty, Beattie gives examples of everyday phrases that promote growth mindsets, and ones that do not. Examples are as follows:

- Praise after success: "You're improving. Your efforts are really paying off" [reinforcing a growth mindset] instead of "You are really good at that!" [reinforcing a fixed mindset]
- Encouragement after difficulty: "Struggling on this assignment doesn't mean you can't get it. It means you're learning it. Your brain is making connections that are not yet strong" [reinforcing a growth mindset] instead of "Well, not everyone could get an A on that test. Just try to do better." [reinforcing a fixed mindset]
- Critical feedback: "This class has a high standard. I wouldn't hold you to it if I didn't believe that together we could get there" [reinforcing a growth mindset] instead of "Well, you may not be good at writing, but you have real strengths in _____." [reinforcing a fixed mindset] (Beattie, 2015)

Dweck (2006) also gives advice on how to promote growth mindsets and examples that are useful in many different settings. In her book *Mindset: The*

New Psychology of Success, she gives readers several techniques for changing a fixed mindset frame to a growth mindset frame. She points out that "just learning about the growth mindset can cause a big shift in the way people think about themselves and their lives" (p. 216). In addition, throughout the book, Dweck has numerous suggestions of responses that we can use when giving feedback, which can add to the examples just given from Beattie (2015). Overall, when giving feedback, the emphasis should be on the students' efforts, focus, and dedication to hard work, not on their ability or how smart they are.

Finally, professors can promote growth mindsets by sharing with students their own story (if they have one). If you had to overcome any academic difficulties or challenges when you were in college, it can be inspiring to your students to hear about it. You can share your story in a short biography that you can post (with your picture) on your class website (Blackboard Learn) or when you introduce yourself to your class at the beginning of the semester. Or it might be later in the semester when an opportunity to share arises. Although at the beginning of one semester I had shared with my students my story about being a "special admit" when I started college, I had another opportunity to share a story later in the semester.

I was working with a small group of at-risk students who needed extra help, and as I was writing some key points on the board, I asked one of the students to check the spelling of a word. Another student, Dennis, spoke up: "Wow. You really aren't a very good speller." I responded, "Yes, that's true. However, I am better than I used to be. I have learned some spelling strategies, and I know how to have someone else check my work—like I just did now." Dennis said, "But, Dr. Gabe, you have your doctorate." "Well, being a poor speller can't keep you from learning and being successful in college," I told him. Then, he shook his head, and after a long pause he slammed his hand on the desk and exclaimed, "You just gave me hope!" It was one of those "aha" teachable moments that we all have experienced, and it was special for both my students and me.

Nilson (1998) found that "students appreciate knowing something about you [their professor] as a professional and a person. A little knowledge about you can help inspire a sense of personal loyalty to you" (p. 22). The kind of interactions I have just described can help promote inspiration as well as growth mindsets, and they can be part of our class sessions and our class meetings.

Mental Toughness

Another way we can help our students is to introduce them to the concepts of mental toughness. Mental toughness is closely related to the growth mindset, but it also includes additional concepts. Mental toughness concepts can be especially beneficial for struggling students, who may face problems beyond having a fixed mindset, which can lead to self-defeating behaviors. These types of behaviors are often not displayed at the beginning of the semester when new students are excited to start college. Thompson and Geren (2002) point out that students "may at first find it easy to adjust to a typical academic load. By midterms, however, students may become overwhelmed, and professors should be especially sensitive to early signs of trouble, such as absenteeism, moodiness, and poor personal hygiene" (p. 399). Students may also start questioning their goals and not have a clear focus on what they hope to accomplish in college.

In another study, Hassel and Lourey (2005) observe that no matter what the goal is for attending college, "many [college students] do not understand what is required to reach the goal, which leads to frustration and apathy" (p. 3). When this happens, students can get farther and farther behind in their class assignments. Many also receive poor grades on early exams or first papers, but having mental toughness can help students get back in control and handle the pressures they are facing instead of falling apart or giving up.

It can be helpful if we are proactive in introducing mental toughness (and mindsets, as discussed previously) to students, because many at-risk students do not share their troubles and often do not seek help or know how to seek it. As Clough and Strycharczyk (2012a) point out, many drowning students don't ask for help; they just drown. Noel, Forsyth, and Kelley (1987) also note that many students do not seek help because they ascribed their poor performance to external and environmental factors that the students believe are beyond their personal control. When this is the case, the students' motivation can waver, and they fail to seek help or "take steps to improve their grades" (p. 152).

To help struggling students, Clough and Strycharczyk (2012a) recommend that we teach them how to help themselves by using concepts of mental toughness. *Mental toughness* is defined as "the quality which determines, in large part, how individuals deal effectively with challenge, stressors, pressure, . . . irrespective of the prevailing circumstances" (2012a, p. 1). It is a quality that is significant for promoting retention and success for any struggling student, but especially for those who historically have not been successful in colleges and universities. Clough and Strycharczyk found that not only does mental toughness relate to resilience and one's inner drive to succeed, but it also is a significant factor in raising completion levels and lowering dropout rates. Furthermore, mental toughness is a life skill that is useful in many other aspects of life, including employability and overall well-being.

In describing and measuring mental toughness, Clough and Strycharczyk (2012a, 2012b) list four components: commitment, challenge, confidence, and control. Following is a brief description of the mental toughness components:

> Commitment . . . describes the ability of an individual to make a "promise" and keep it (including promises to themselves), despite any problems or setbacks that arise while achieving the goal . . . . Challenge describes the extent to which individual[s] see challenge and problems or opportunities . . . . Confidence [is] . . . the self-belief to complete successfully tasks that may be considered too difficult by individuals with similar abilities but lower confidence. (Clough & Strycharczyk, 2012b, pp. 78–79)

Finally, control refers to the extent to which people feel they are in control of "their studies, work, and environment in which they work" (Clough & Strycharczyk, 2012b, p. 77).

Similar to having a growth mindset, Clough and Strycharczyk (2012a) found that mental toughness can be a quality that students already have, but it, too, can be nurtured and developed. With interventions and coaching, students can develop their own mental toughness, and professors can play an essential role in making this happen. Clough and Strycharczyk give suggestions that professors can incorporate into their class and teaching methods, which I discuss next.

Nurturing Mental Toughness Components

For each of the four components of mental toughness, the following recommendations are ways professors can incorporate interventions for their students in order to promote success for all the students in their classes, especially those who have traditionally been unsuccessful.

Commitment

Clough and Strycharczyk (2012a) have found that professors can assist students in recognizing the importance of making a commitment to be engaged and put forth their best effort to accomplish the learning outcomes for the class. The first intervention, or coaching moment, can begin on the first day of class when we ask students to make a commitment to complete the class. (See chapter 3 for further discussion.) Stick-ability, or stick-to-itiveness, is a part of making a commitment, in that students are making a promise and plan to stick with it for the entire semester. This sets a goal, and students must affirmatively say to themselves that they will go for it, work hard and not give up even when the going gets tough, and seek help when needed. *Resilience* is often defined as a function of commitment, because it refers to being able to handle, or deal with, an adverse situation and still complete some or all of what one had set out to do (Clough & Strycharczyk, 2012a). Hence, it is fulfilling one's commitment. This action has been especially helpful for first-generation and academically unprepared students because part of the commitment is to seek help when they are struggling.

Challenge

Challenge is another component of mental toughness as defined by Clough and Strycharczyk (2012a). If students view challenges as a threat, and not as an opportunity, then they might have high anxiety, trouble concentrating, or difficulty staying engaged with the task at hand. One way to intervene with these students is to invite them to meet with us individually so that we can discuss the challenges they may have in mastering the material or completing assignments.

At class meetings, simply asking for sign-ups for office-hour meetings (or for other times if a student cannot make your office hours) will increase the number of students who come to your office hours. I have found that it helps to pass around a clipboard during class with my office-hour times broken into 15-minute blocks so that students can sign up to meet either individually or in small groups. When meeting with students at our offices, or even at the student union (or cafeteria on campus) for coffee, we can listen to their individual worries or concerns. To respond, Clough and Strycharczyk (2012b) suggest that professors can help students remember other challenges that they have overcome in the past or urge them to build on existing or forgotten personal strengths and attributes. In doing so, we—the professors to whom students often look for encouragement—are nurturing our students' mental toughness, which, in turn, can improve their performance, engagement, retention, and persistence.

It is important to ensure that individual or small group meetings can actually occur. Many professors and instructors can attest to sitting all alone during their office hours because no one shows up. In response to using e-mail as an alternative, some universities and colleges have even decreased the number of office hours that faculty are required to have. McClenney (2004) reminds us that many of the diverse students we serve "have significant time commitments to their families, their jobs, and their communities in addition to their studies" (p. 2). Thus, contact outside of class time likely will not happen by chance, so we must also plan for ways to make it happen. Some professors have a "requirement" that at least once during the semester students must meet with them outside of class, and they will have students sign up during class time for a specific appointment time and day.

Of course, as the professor, one must be willing to meet at times outside of the scheduled office hours (using "To Be Arranged" times). I do not require this type of meeting but offer "bonus" points for a first-time meeting with me during the first six weeks of the semester (Gabriel, 2008). Furthermore, after the initial meeting, most students will return throughout the semester. Sadigh (2016) found that initiating contact for a meeting outside of class with a simple "Please see me" at the top of a returned paper or test goes a long way: "Notably, those who met with me began to do better on future tests; their assignments improved as well" (p. 1). This professor was able to assist students who were at first too embarrassed about their poor performance to see her and those who did not understand what had gone wrong. Sadigh notes:

I made every attempt to make it clear to them that we were going to work together to find a way to improve their performance . . . . Our office meetings help students learn that it's OK to openly explore and discuss their concerns, doubts, and fears. Rather than avoiding their problems, they learn that reaching out and sharing their concerns is the first step to breaking down the barriers that are holding them back. This is a skill that will serve them well throughout their lives. They also discover their profs are real people. (p. 1)

Meeting with small groups can also help, especially if you have limited time to meet with individual students. Small group meetings are also helpful when discussing study or learning strategies, or clarifying assignments. Even though these topics are introduced in class, being available for consultation outside of class can be a crucial component in helping struggling students get back on track. Just as in promoting growth mindsets, in nurturing mental toughness faculty availability is essential for increasing student retention, persistence, and graduation rates (Seidman, 2012; Seymour & Hewitt, 1997; Tinto, 1997b).

Confidence

When considering the confidence component of mental toughness, we must consider the fixed and growth mindsets discussed previously. There are similarities because confidence is directly related to the belief in one's ability to deal with what will be faced. Students may ask themselves, "Do I have the capability to plow on?" and how confident they are can impact their answer. Confidence also impacts how students will deal with setbacks. In addition,

Clough and Strycharczyk (2012a) discuss having interpersonal confidence, which is having the inner strength to stand one's own ground when needed. Bueschel (2008) points out that this area is important not only for those who are academically unprepared, but also for diverse students—minorities and first-generation students—"who are likely to lack self-confidence as learners and fear failure" (p. 6).

Clough and Strycharczyk (2012a) note that teaching students positive thinking (e.g., "You can do this") and using positive affirmations are effective interventions when students have low confidence. One message that is especially important for academically unprepared students to hear is that they will need to work hard (and long hours). To have such a frank and honest approach from the beginning can help students realize just how essential their own determination is to their own success. I often reinforce this message with a "Quote of the Week" (described previously). In addition, I use quotes that refer to the importance and power of obtaining an education. These are especially helpful along with quotes that encourage one to never give up and to work hard even when progress seems out of reach. (See Appendix C for additional examples of quotes.)

Several times during the semester, I substitute a weekly quote with a short (less-than-one-minute) video clip that has a message that supports either a growth mindset or mental toughness. One I often show approximately a third of the way into the semester is Michael Jordan's (2012) *Michael Jordan "Failure" Commercial.* He narrates this 34-second clip, in which he lists many of his failures, and his last sentence is, "I have failed over and over and over again in my life . . . and that is why I succeed." Jordan's message to keep trying even after failing can help students build their own confidence.

Another video clip that I show is Misty Copeland's (n.d.) *Under Armour—Misty Copeland—I Will What I Want.* Copeland is the first African American female principal dancer with the prestigious American Ballet Theatre. In the clip, the narrator reads a letter that Copeland received when she was a young girl rejecting her application to the ballerina school. The video shows her "triumphing" over the rejection. Copeland grew up very poor with plenty of hard times, and her story is truly inspirational with a message to work hard to follow one's dream.

Control

The last component of mental toughness is control. Control also has two parts: life control and emotional control. Overall, control refers to the extent that students believe they can shape what happens to them and how they can manage or control their emotions as they go through various situations.

Having a strong or high-level attitude of being in control does not mean that these students think problems or unfortunate things will not happen to them, but rather that they can handle these issues and manage their emotional responses to them (Clough & Strycharczyk, 2012a). Clough and Strycharczyk also found that students with a low sense of control often blame others and circumstances for their own failures and often focus on why things can not be done. These students tend to get down when things go wrong and are more susceptible to "giving up."

When fostering mental toughness, and in particular the aspect of control, Clough and Strycharczyk (2012a) recommend suggesting to students who are feeling overwhelmed that they try talking themselves through it with statements such as, "This feeling will fade away and won't last forever" or "I know how to control these feelings. I must concentrate on relaxing myself" (p. 216).

Using affirmations, thinking about positive outcomes, and turning negative statements into positive ones are additional ways for students to help themselves gain a stronger feeling of control. Relaxation and breathing techniques can also help with anxiety control, and these techniques can be posted on class web pages or discussed in and out of class.

A longer (a little over six minutes), powerful video that I also sometimes show is a TED Talk titled *Grit: The Power of Passion and Perseverance* by Angela Lee Duckworth (2013). If you do not want to take up class time to show this video, it can be a homework assignment. In this video, Duckworth emphasizes the importance of being able to cope with all the pressures and difficulties that occur in one's life. Students who have the mental grit to cope with these challenges are "less likely to leave college before graduating" (Bean & Eaton, 2000, p. 51).

For professors who would like to "assess" their students' mental toughness, Clough and Strycharczyk (2012a) designed an assessment questionnaire, the MTQ48, that students can take:

> The MTQ48 measures are robust and practical developments which provide coaches and mentors in education with a structure and accessible way to attend to a key need in the development of young people: to guide them in learning how to deal with challenges as well as dealing with the stressors and pressures of growing up and optimizing their involvement with the education process. (p. 90)

Self-Efficacy Reinforced

The principles of a growth mindset and of mental toughness are related to self-efficacy. Simply put, self-efficacy refers to "people's belief about their capabilities to produce effects" (Bandura, 1994, p. 72). Having a growth mindset increases students' certainty that they can improve and increase their own "learning" power. Also, people with strong self-efficacy will have confidence in their ability to manage their own motivation and their own behavior (Bandura, 1994). Therefore, growth mindsets and mental toughness promote students' self-efficacy and vice versa.

Bandura (1994) points out that it is advantageous for students to create and strengthen their own "self-beliefs of efficacy," and one way to do this "is through vicarious experiences provided by social models. Seeing people similar to oneself succeed by sustained effort raises observers' beliefs that they too possess the capabilities by mastering comparable activities to succeed" (p. 73). Many historically underrepresented students, including those who are minority, low income, first generation, and academically underprepared, do not "see" themselves fitting in on campus or in their classes. This can be especially true for minority students at predominantly White institutions. Bandura (1994) explains: "If people see the models as very different from themselves, their perceived self-efficacy is not much influenced by the models' behavior and the results it produces" (p. 73).

Knowing this, we can increase the diversity of the "models" that students observe by taking pictures of our diverse students and posting these pictures on our class web page (e.g., Blackboard Learn) and in our offices. As students are participating in various activities (e.g., working in small groups, voting with cards, presenting or working at the board), I take casual pictures. It is pretty easy to do with an iPad or smartphone (or even have students take pictures for you). I ask students to sign a permission slip so I can post their pictures, and I have never had a student turn me down. Most tell me they are honored to have their picture posted, especially when I frame and put those pictures in my office. When appropriate, I include some of their pictures as part of my PowerPoint slides throughout the semester. Students can "see" themselves and fellow students in the pictures engaged in academic pursuits with looks of seriousness and smiles on their faces. When students graduate, I take more formal pictures of them in their caps and gowns and frame and hang some of them in my office.

Professors can take pictures of those who are currently in class, who are majoring in the professor's field, and who graduated from that field. For students who are just starting out, these examples can be very motivating. We all have had students who had to overcome obstacles and challenges, made tremendous progress, and then made it to graduation. Displaying pictures of these students who persevered can inspire others. Several of my students shared with me that the pictures in my office made them feel like they belonged, not just as part of the class, but as part of the college. At the end of his junior year, one of my students revealed the following to me:

> When I first got here, my freshman year was tough. I just didn't think I would ever get thru [*sic*] and even in my second year, I didn't think I would ever graduate. But, when I came in your office and saw graduation pictures of some guys that I know on your wall, I knew I could make it. I said to myself, If Raymond and Webster can do this—so can I. So, next year, when I graduate—I can't wait to see my picture on your wall!

Over the years, I have found the pictures to be a vital—albeit small—part of my courses and office setting by contributing to a hospitable, personal, and inclusive atmosphere. Having pictures of one's students also demonstrates the professor's interest in the students as individuals—not just as interchangeable students passing through from year to year. Several studies have shown that when professors show a personal interest and have a positive attitude toward their students, the students' motivation and attendance increase (Gabriel, 2008; Jaasma & Koper, 1999; Sleigh, Ritzer, & Casey, 2002). Both of these attributes are directly related to engagement and learning.

In addition, professors can include pictures of many different and diverse people from our field who are accomplished and excellent role models to help promote our students' self-efficacy (see chapters 2 and 3). Having diverse guest speakers, including those who graduated from your program or major and are now in the field, can also be a valuable and stimulating experience for students.

As we reinforce growth mindsets and mental toughness, our message should include having high expectations to work hard, persevere, and learn how to use learning strategies. As Tinto (2012) reminds us, "Expectations matter for student success" (p. 24). Finally, we know that for historically underserved students facing many obstacles and challenges, their own determination and educational aspirations can make a difference in their ability to overcome the odds of failure (Kuh, Kinzie, et al., 2007).

Self-efficacy is a beneficial characteristic for professors. Alder (1990) notes that teachers with a high sense of efficacy are the ones who are the most successful in reaching low-achieving students. These teachers have "confidence in their ability to influence student learning and motivation . . . . [They are] more likely to view low-achieving students as reachable, teachable, and worthy of their attention and effort (Alder, 1990, p. 28). When professors recognize that most of these students can make tremendous improvements in college and communicate these high expectations, students come to understand that the professors are there to assist them as long as they, the students, are also willing to put forth the time, energy, and sustained effort.

Conclusion

Struggling students who display self-defeating behaviors often do so because they do not really know how to turn the tide and frequently believe that they will not be able to do so. Faculty may display negative attitudes and an unwillingness to assist such students if they believe it is too late for the students to make significant academic gains. Notions such as "They should have learned this in high school" may be true, but this attitude does not help the students or the professors. Fortunately, there are alternatives.

Promoting growth mindsets and nurturing mental toughness are especially useful because we can empower students as they navigate their way through college. We can encourage them to continually improve and reach our high expectations and standards, and at the same time provide support. As Laird and colleagues (2008) note, "Everyone agrees that persistence and educational attainment rates, as well as the quality of student learning, must improve if postsecondary education is to meet the needs of our nation and the rest of the world" (p. 85). By using different interventions to promote growth mindsets, nurture mental toughness, and increase self-efficacy, professors can help close the achievement gaps among the different students enrolled in our courses.

Note

1. Visit https://www.cpp.edu/~lsstarkey/courses/GrowYourBrainArticle-Carnegie.pdf for complete article. Also visit https://www.broward.edu/sacs/qep/SiteAssets/Lists/Learning%20Activities/EditForm/Learning_Activity_based_on_Growth_Mindset.pdf for an article with questions for students to answer.

5

INTERACTIVE LECTURES

Using Meaningful Educational Activities

*To bring about change, you must not be afraid to take the
first step. We will fail when we fail to try.*

—*Rosa Parks (1913–2005)*

Introduction

Tinto (1997a) reminds us that "at its core, college is an educational experience . . . . Conversations about persistence that ignore important questions of educational practice are conversations that are at best shallow" (p. 620). The educational practices professors implement in their classrooms factor into student retention, persistence, and success. This chapter examines the practice of using lectures and interactive lectures.

The educational practice of professors lecturing (or presenting) to students has been around for a long time. The traditional lecture has been portrayed in several ways: a time-honored tradition for delivering instruction and information to the students, "a century-old staple of the college classroom, [and] . . . . an unavoidable feature of our education" (Barone, 2016, p. 1). Indeed, most administrators, deans, and professors find it acceptable to regard their teaching responsibility "as primarily delivering 50-minute lectures" several times a week (Barr & Tagg, 1995, p. 13).

Lectures are still the most widely used teaching technique for undergraduate courses whether it is a face-to-face setting (live performance) or an online class (prerecorded lecture uploaded to the school's website). Colleges and universities can save money by setting up very large classes for undergraduates,[1] and in many cases, for economic reasons, there is a push for online courses. In both situations, the traditional lecture is not only used but also reinforced.

However, delivering lectures is a teaching method that "is contrary to almost every principle of optimal settings for student learning" (Guskin as cited in Barr & Tagg, 1995, p. 13). Because of the prevalence of lecture use, Chickering and Kuh (2005) note that other effective educational practices are underutilized. According to Barr and Tagg (1995), "The more we discover about how the mind works and how students learn, the greater the disparity between what we say and what we do" (p. 14). We say we want our students to be engaged in their learning and to participate in class, but still the majority of professors lecture while students have a passive and inactive role—listening, taking notes, and rarely raising their hand to be called on if they have a question. If engagement creates a path to success in the classroom, then we, as professors, can choose not to continue using a straight traditional lecture method where the pathway is narrowed.

The persistence of the lecture may in part be attributable to the belief that teaching is just not a priority, but competes with requirements to complete research, publish, and write grants. These activities take up much of our time and focus. They are tasks that can reward us with prestige and job security (e.g., earning tenure, promotions, and salary raises) (Kolowich, 2014; Sperber, 2005; R. Talbert, 2014).

Furthermore, many professors confess they do not know how to revise their lecture methods to incorporate the use of "pedagogical innovations to enrich student learning" (Chickering & Kuh, 2005, p. 1). Taking time to learn how to make changes can be viewed as an insurmountable obstacle (R. Talbert, 2014), and there is often not much pressure to do so. Indeed, some claim that colleges and universities are "research flagships and their lecture halls remain in good standing with regulators, accreditors, and prospective students" (Kolowich, 2014, p. 4). If this is the case, there is not much motivation for changing the stand-and-deliver traditional lecture.

Nevertheless, if we value all of our students, we should attend to research results showing that lecturing favors certain student groups to the detriment of others. Beyond describing that research, I discuss practical ways to create interactive lectures and address techniques and tips for effective short lectures along with the use of PowerPoints, class notes, and handouts.

Making lectures interactive with the infusion of meaningful educational activities is not as time-consuming as one might think, and by making a few changes, many readers will be surprised at the strides in learning that students will demonstrate. Class meetings can be an exciting and effective learning time for the students, and equally so for us as the teachers. It is up to us to make this happen.

Favoritism and Bias of the Traditional Lecture Format

Even though the traditional lecture is considered a "main staple" of higher education, if we are truly concerned with student learning, then we, the professors, along with our administrators, college advisers, and even accreditors, should review the evidence about the impact of traditional lectures compared to the results from courses using active learning techniques. When active learning techniques are incorporated into the classroom, all students benefit. Reason and colleagues (2006) note that requiring students to actively engage with the course content "produced greater gains in learning and cognitive skill development than did the more traditional lecture [or the lecture–whole-class discussion method]" (p. 155). Kinzie and colleagues (2008) also found that "student engagement had a positive, statistically significant effect on persistence, even after controlling for background characteristics, other college experiences during the first college year, academic achievement, and financial aid" (p. 26). Using active and collaborative learning approaches in the classroom is an important part of shaping all student behaviors, but particularly for historically underrepresented and academically unprepared students.

Eddy and Hogan's (2014) study reveals that a traditional lecture course does have a positive impact for some students. Disaggregating the data, they also found that traditional lectures not only favor a higher learning performance for White, affluent, male students but also are biased against minority, first-generation, women, and academically unprepared students. In their extensive four-year study, Eddy and Hogan disaggregated the student achievement data by race, gender, and first-generation and continuing-generation categories to see how different groups performed in a traditional lecture class (low structure) versus a moderately structured class that had some active learning activities. The low-structure class had little student participation during class because it was all lecture, and there were three homework assignments designed to help students prepare for the three exams. The moderately structured class not only had some in-class activities but also had outside homework assignments that were graded. The homework included guided-reading questions, a few preparatory assignments, and a few review assignments. Eddy and Hogan's study included different instructors, different courses (subjects), and different student bodies.

The results showed that for classes with in-class engagement activities, performance was increased for all students. More important, when considering the differences between Black and White students, males and females, and first-generation and continuing-generation students, the achievement gap was significantly reduced or closed (Eddy & Hogan, 2014). In addition to increased exam performance, Black students, female students, and first-generation students spent more time each week on class material both inside and outside of class, participated more in class, and reported a stronger sense of classroom community.

Differences in class participation between Black and White students that existed in traditional lecture classes completely disappeared in classes that moderately used active learning methods. Eddy and Hogan (2014) note that intervention of engagement activities "increased course performance for all student populations, but worked disproportionately well for black students—halving the black–white achievement gap—and first-generation students—closing the achievement gap with continuing-generation students" (p. 453).

In their research, Kuh, Cruce, Shoup, Kinzie, and Gonyea (2007) also report that engagement in the classroom has a "compensatory effect" for grades and persistence by "increasing the odds that they [historically under-represented students] will complete their program of study" (p. 71). Academic performance (revealed by student grades) is crucial for retention and graduation because "course completion patterns (drops, withdrawals, incomplete grades or repeats) are a drag on bachelor completion rates of students at four-year colleges" (Kinzie et al., 2008, p. 29).

Paul (2015) agrees that the continued use of a traditional straight lecture "offers unfair advantages to an already privileged population" (p. 1). Yet, every one of us can use interactive lectures in class to level the playing field. "The classroom is one key arena, if not the only one available, for unprepared students to participate in powerful, meaningful learning opportunities" (Engstrom, 2008, p. 7).

Creating Interactive Lectures

Implementing interactive lectures does not mean sacrificing academic rigor. It also does not mean that lectures have to be abolished, or that they are "no longer an appropriate instructional approach" (Kinzie et al., 2008, p. 31). What it does require is breaking up a lecture to incorporate meaningful educational activities that engage students to allow them to interact as they discuss, reflect, relate, scrutinize, evaluate, and/or apply their understanding of the course material and issues. This practice is often referred to as "activity learning," and it "puts into practice over a half-century of research that demonstrates that to truly learn, we need to make an idea, a concept, or a solution our own by working it into our personal knowledge and experience" (Barkley, 2009, p. 16).

Tinto (2012) uses the term *pedagogies of engagement*. He explains: "Unlike the traditional lecture, where students are typically passive, especially in many large first-year classrooms that dot the postsecondary landscape, pedagogies of engagement require students to be actively engaged in learning with other students in the classroom" (p. 68). Some professors have shared that they feel a little nervous about using pedagogies of engagement and, in particular, about giving an "interactive lecture" in lieu of their traditional lecture. Giving interactive lectures may seem challenging, but by using the following five steps, interactive lectures can easily be created and much of the presentation material one already has can still be used:

1. Time all activities and lecture components at every class meeting.
2. Build in individual accountability by "grading" class activities.
3. Keep the activities purposeful, meaningful, and relevant.
4. Vary the "level of learning" of the tasks and provide feedback.
5. Start with only one or two activities and then, when ready, scale up.

Time All Activities and Lecture Components at Every Class Meeting

Interactive lectures are simply lectures that have breaks within the class meeting time to give students opportunities to interact with the professor and with classmates in meaningful educational activities. Lecturing for most of the class period (e.g., the first 40 to 45 minutes) followed by an engaging activity for the last 5 or 10 minutes of class does not really constitute an interactive lecture and generally does not work well. Considering the extensive research on attention span for listening to lectures, Wankat (2002) notes that "50 minutes of straight lecture does not work" (p. 68) and suggests that professors limit their lecture to 15 to 20 minutes at the most, and even consider 10-minute minilectures as an option.

During class, we must manage the clock so that we are adhering to Chickering and Gamson's (1987) fifth principle of good practice for undergraduate education, which emphasizes time-on-task. They note, "Time plus energy equals learning. There is no substitute for time-on-task. Learning to use one's time well is critical for students and professors alike" (p. 5). To ensure our students will not view class time as wasted time, we must be diligent in timing all class activities, including our own talking or lecture time. If one or two students in our class need extra help, rather then letting them sidetrack the class agenda, we can ask them to see us after class for extra assistance.

As professors, when we use a timer, it is easier to stick to the time limits. When the timer goes off, we can stop lecturing (even if behind in our presentation notes) and have the students complete an engaging activity (several options are described in the following section). Then, for the activity, the timer should be set again, and again for the next part of the lecture. By having a timer, many professors have noted that they can manage their time more effectively, and it also helps in planning the structure of the class. For a 50-minute class period, the structure can be organized in different ways; I recommend always ending with focused attention on the professor for class wrap-up. Following are a few examples of different structures for an interactive lecture:

- Example One: 15-minute opening lecture, 15-minute activity, 10-minute lecture, 5-minute activity, 5-minute lecture with class wrap-up
- Example Two: 10-minute lecture, 2-minute activity, 15-minute lecture, 3-minute activity, 10-minute lecture, 5-minute activity, 5-minute lecture with closing wrap-up
- Example Three: 5-minute opening activity, 20-minute lecture, 5-minute activity, 20-minute lecture with class wrap-up

There are numerous additional ways that professors can structure their interactive lecture. In the previous examples, the class activity time ranges from 10 to 20 minutes of the 50-minute class period, but it can be more. Additionally, an attention signal will need to be set up so that students will know when the activity time expires, and students' attention is to be directed back to the professor for the next part of the lecture.

Once an attention signal is taught, students will also quickly recognize it and respond accordingly. For example, for large or small classes, professors can very quickly teach students the "raised arm or hand" signal:

> The professor is to tell the students that when the time is up, the professor will raise his/her hand. As soon as anyone in the room sees a hand up, s/he is to raise her or his hand. All hands are to remain raised until the entire room is quiet. When using this technique, I have the class practice it before the "sharing" begins. (Gabriel, 2008, p. 94)

After each activity, most students' attention span is reset, and they are ready to pay attention to another short lecture. The interactive lecture is a learner-centered pedagogy, and for consistency and continuous engagement, the interactive lecture, or variation thereof, should be used for every single class meeting. The vast majority of students will quickly respond to the expectations of being present and engaged for each class.

Build In Individual Accountability by "Grading" Class Activities

Individual accountability is a must; therefore, the in-class activities must be part of the students' final grade. Price (2013) points out, "Students consistently report that they are more motivated to adopt behaviors that will positively impact their grade . . . . Assigning work that is not linked to the grade can send the message that the work doesn't matter." Thus, when in-class activities result in points that are part of the final grade, individual accountability is built in, and this practice also increases class attendance.

In addition, Eddy and Hogan (2014) found that "accountability is essential for changing student behaviors" (p. 466). From their research, they report that grading engagement activities is essential. By being counted as part of the final grade, the class activities have added value, even though they are valuable on their own merit.

How one chooses to grade the in-class activities varies; collecting and scoring written work that each student completes before, during, or after the class activity is effective. For example, for a Write-Pair-Share activity, I give students a prompt, and then about 60 to 90 seconds to write their response on a 3-inch-by-5-inch card. Depending on the question or prompt, another minute or so can be added to the writing time. Then, in small groups of 2 or 3 students, students share their responses for 2 to 3 minutes. After groups have had time to talk, I randomly call on 3 or 4 students to share their own response or what someone in their group said. Finally, students turn in their cards. After class, I score the cards with a check plus, a check, or a check minus. However, the class activity is always worth points that go toward the "class activities" portion of the final grade.

Because their response cards are not graded like a "formal" paper, points are awarded for good effort in the information and a demonstration of the student's reflection. As Barkley (2009) notes, "Active learning means that *the mind* is actively engaged. Its defining characteristics are that students are dynamic participants in their learning and that they are reflecting on and monitoring both the processes and the results of their learning" (p. 17). I do not give any points for responses that are off topic, superficial, or obviously lack reflection. However, even if a student is confused, he or she can receive full points for that activity, and I will ask the student to see me after class. Scored cards are returned to the students within a week.

Although I recommend having interactive lectures for every class meeting, I do not always collect written responses. However, it is important to move around the room to make sure that everyone is participating in their small groups. I will write down the names of those who are not in class or not participating, and everyone else will receive full points. One class period, I saw three students just sitting in their small group not talking to each other. I quietly told them they were not earning their class activity points because they were not doing the assigned activity. Immediately there was a change. I gave them partial points for that day, but their "disengaged" behavior did not happen again that semester.

Finally, it is important to mix up the small groups throughout the semester, so that students are not interacting with the same people for each class. Reason and colleagues (2006) found that academic endeavors are enhanced when students have increased levels of engagement "with new ideas and people [who are] in some way different from themselves" (p. 155). Furthermore, coming into contact with "diverse people, cultures and ideas [is a] . . . powerful predictor of growth in academic competence" (Reason et al., 2006, p. 170). (See chapter 2 and Appendix B for examples of how to organize multiple small groups.)

Keep the Activities Purposeful, Meaningful, and Relevant

When designing an interactive lecture, the class activities part should relate to the class and/or subject matter directly or indirectly. "We need to use meaningful educational tasks to allow students to write, share, report, or solve problems" (Gabriel, 2008, p. 53). For student motivation, it is imperative to explain the relevancy of the activities to the course material and learning objectives; it is also important to include moral, ethical, and real-world issues for class activities. (See chapter 3 for further discussion.)

Some class activities might take the form of a guided practice where students have an in-depth exploration of key concepts. Application of material to real-world tasks is another example of a class activity that supports the relevancy of what the students are doing with the course content. Price (2013) points out that "millennial learners, in particular, report a need to understand how learning will link to their real lives. Spending time creating [activities or] assignments that are clearly linked to current or future life activities will pay off in greater student attention and motivation." Having students consider case studies and propose solutions to challenging scenarios are excellent examples of educationally purposeful activities in which students must grasp and apply the content of the course material.

In the famous "Seven Principles for Good Practice in Undergraduate Education," Chickering and Gamson (1987) list "encourages active learning" as the third principle. They note that students "must talk about what they are learning, write about it, relate it to past experiences and apply it to their daily lives. They must make what they learn part of themselves" (p. 4). Having structured exercises during class is an excellent way to give students opportunities to inquire, appraise, compare, predict, and differentiate—to name a few ways for them to analyze and synthesize the course material. This also gives students a chance to work with people from different backgrounds. Eddy and Hogan (2014) report that with consistent use of structured in-class activities—especially when the activities involved small groups working together in a more collaborative way—students developed a sense of belonging, and when students have a feeling that they are "part of a community . . . [this] increases both performance and motivation, especially for historically underrepresented groups" (p. 456).

Finally, class activities should not be viewed as busywork, or just a way to entertain or liven up the class. To have students ready for in-class activities, professors should consider assigning preparatory or review assignments that students bring to class and then are used to complete the class activity. As Kinzie and colleagues (2008) point out, because we have an "increasingly diverse student population, it is necessary to make clear the demands of academic work and spell out what students need to do" (p. 11). The preactivities along with in-class activities help students spend time on the course material throughout the entire semester and can prevent the practice of simply cramming just before the final exam (Eddy & Hogan, 2014). For example, if students are assigned guided-reading questions in between exams and these assignments are graded, not only will students complete these assignments, which are part of their total grade, but these activities will also help prepare them for the exam. (For additional examples of proactive assignments, see chapters 6 and 7.)

Vary the level of learning of the tasks and provide feedback. McGuire (2015) notes that to help students develop learning goals (as opposed to grade point average goals) and become aware of ways to improve their own learning, we need to introduce them to metacognition and Bloom's Taxonomy. Basically, metacognition is the process of thinking about one's own thinking. When students use metacognition,

> they become consciously aware of themselves as problem solvers, which enables them to actively seek solutions to any problems they may encounter, rather than relying on others to tell them what to do or to answer their questions. As they make the transition from being passive learners to proactive learners, students gain ability to monitor, plan and control their own mental processing. (McGuire, 2015, p. 16)

After introducing students to the metacognition concept, McGuire (2015) then teaches them about Bloom's Taxonomy. Bloom's Taxonomy is a hierarchy of learning levels, beginning with knowledge (the lowest and simplest learning level) followed by comprehension, application, analysis, synthesis, and finally evaluation (the highest and most complex level of learning). Students are also given definitions and examples of each level of learning (Figure 5.1).

Once students understand Bloom's Taxonomy, they can judge the level of learning they are (or have been) using as they receive and grasp the course material. Many students will realize that they may be operating only at the knowledge level and not moving to deeper levels of learning. We can also

Figure 5.1. Bloom's Taxonomy and definitions.

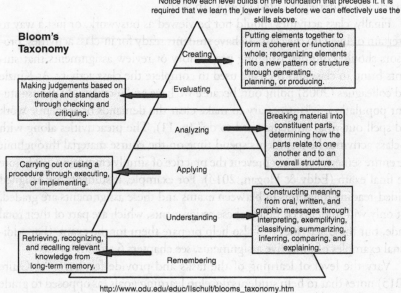

This pyramid depicts the different levels of thinking we use when learning. Notice how each level builds on the foundation that precedes it. it is required that we learn the lower levels before we can effectively use the skills above.

Bloom's Taxonomy

Creating — Putting elements together to form a coherent or functional whole; reorganizing elements into a new pattern or structure through generating, planning, or producing.

Evaluating — Making judgements based on criteria and standards through checking and critiquing.

Analyzing — Breaking material into constituent parts, determining how the parts relate to one another and to an overall structure.

Applying — Carrying out or using a procedure through executing, or implementing.

Understanding — Constructing meaning from oral, written, and graphic messages through interpreting, exemplifying, classifying, summarizing, inferring, comparing, and explaining.

Remembering — Retrieving, recognizing, and recalling relevant knowledge from long-term memory.

http://www.odu.edu/educ/llschult/blooms_taxonomy.htm

Note. Adapted with permission from "Image of Revised Versions of Bloom's Taxonomy Featuring Definitions," by R. Overbaugh, n.d.

help students by designing the engagement activities for different levels—tasks from remembering, to understanding, to applying, to analyzing, and so on. In addition, as students complete different "meaningful and purposeful" educational tasks, we, their professors, can provide feedback so that they can refine their learning.

By using different levels of learning from Bloom's Taxonomy, we can also vary the challenges we create for our students. As Barkley (2009) reminds us, "If a learning task is too easy, it can become boring; if a learning task is too hard, it can become frustrating. Either extremes [*sic*] can lead to disengagement" (p. 127). Our classrooms comprise students with a wide range of prior knowledge and experience, so varying the challenge and/or difficulty of class activities is crucial to keep everyone engaged. Kinzie and colleagues (2008) conclude, "In particular, what faculty do in terms of structuring engaging opportunities into their courses, coupled with a healthy measure of prompt feedback, are essential to shaping . . . desirable student academic performance" (p. 34). (See chapter 7 for further discussion on feedback.)

Start with only one or two activities and then, when ready, scale up. *Active learning* is an umbrella term that now refers to several models of instruction, including cooperative and collaborative learning, discovery learning, experiential learning, problem-based learning and inquiry-based learning" (Barkley, 2009, p. 16). There are many ways we can incorporate active learning techniques in our classrooms, such as Write-Pair-Share, voting on issues, application cards, and ranking and matching, to name a few. However, to start using interactive lectures in one's course, you do not have to use all these activities. Whether you are a new first-year faculty member or a seasoned tenured professor, you might be a novice when it comes to creating an interactive lecture. My advice is to start simply with only one or two activities, and once you feel comfortable, expand.

Two activities that are fairly easy to incorporate have already been discussed: Write-Pair-Share (discussed previously), and the Gallery Walk (discussed in chapter 3). Either can be used in different ways for different learning levels. For a variation of the Write-Pair-Share, the students first can pair up to discuss their responses and even use their textbooks to look up information and then write their individual responses.

For the Gallery Walk, instead of having topics listed, images or graphs can be taped in the middle of the different poster papers. The images can be directly or indirectly related to the material being covered, and the written responses of the students can be on the posters or on individual response papers. Students can be asked to compare and contrast, integrate, and analyze the relationships of the different images.

Collaborative learning and team-based learning are also excellent educational activities. For my education classes (in a teacher preparation program), I give students real-life scenarios. For instance, I give the example of a young person who has a behavior and learning problem and the parents' reaction to the child's problem and how their child is performing at school. Next, using their text and lecture material, the students have to discuss possible steps that might be taken to address the problem. After students work in small groups of three people, they write out their answers. Finally, we have a whole-class discussion, which is usually pretty lively. Sometimes I take on the role of devil's advocate and role-play the administrator or parent whom the future teachers may have to face.

Having students vote on multiple-choice questions that are posted on a PowerPoint slide is another engaging activity. This can be done using electronic clickers or color-coded voting index cards. Often students vote on their own, but what really gets them involved is when they have to talk to a classmate about their answers (Gabriel, 2008). A variation of this activity is to put students in teams of three to four and give them a set of large cards of different colors representing the possible answers (A, B, C, or D or True [T] or False [F]). For example, cards representing answer "A" might be green and those representing answer "B" might be red.

When a question is asked, the groups must discuss their answers. "At a given signal, one person from each team displays the team's answer, allowing the instructor to determine how well students understood the question" (Mills, 2012, p. 1). Then, the professor can review the correct and incorrect answers but also can call on different groups "to explain the rationale for their selection, sometimes uncovering misconceptions or poorly constructed, ambiguous wording in the questions" (Mills, 2012, p. 1).

There are many more activities. (See chapter 6 for further discussion on activities using assigned reading from the textbook.)

Finally, don't feel obliged to try all of the different activities that are suggested. Some may not work for you. The important thing is to get started with these types of engaging activities (if you haven't done so already). By using the five steps just discussed, interactive lectures can be created with meaningful educational activities. The interactive lecture supports Astin's theory of involvement in which "learning will be greatest when the learning environment is structured to encourage active participation by the student" (Astin, 1999, as cited in Kuh et al., 2007, p. 522).

Improving Lecture Techniques

While using an interactive lecture may limit the time devoted to imparting content, the techniques that we use for lecturing are still important. Just having a shorter "lecture" does not automatically improve our delivery or how students will benefit. Short lectures (20 minutes or less) can be effective, but they also can be ineffective. Wood (1998) researched the lecture techniques and how different techniques can impact student learning. In particular, Wood found that how we lecture, or techniques used, can affect our students' attention, motivation, and recall of what we present to them.

Specifically, Wood's (1998) study focused on the enthusiasm and structure professors use when delivering lectures and how students responded to these attributes. Five specific teacher behaviors during a lecture were examined: clarity, enthusiasm, pacing, organization, and speech. Each of these behaviors was then evaluated using multiple factors as follows:

- **Clarity factors:** "Gives several examples . . . uses concrete examples . . . fails to define new terms [a negative attribute] . . . repeats difficult ideas . . . stresses important points" (p. 215)
- **Enthusiasm factors:** "Speaks in a 'dramatic way' . . . moves about while lecturing . . . gestures with hands and arms [varies facial expressions] . . . avoids eye contact [a negative attribute] [or has good

eye contact] . . . tells jokes [or uses humor] . . . reads lecture verbatim [a negative attribute] . . . smiles or laughs; distracting mannerisms [a negative attribute]" (p. 215)

- **Pacing factors:** "Dwells excessively on obvious points [a negative attribute] . . . digresses from major theme [a negative attribute] . . . covers too much material [a negative attribute] . . . [appropriate pacing and pauses for important points]" (p. 216)
- **Organization factors:** "Gives preliminary overview . . . puts outline on blackboard [chalk or white board] . . . uses heading and subheadings . . . clearly indicates transitions . . . periodically summarizes" (p. 216)
- **Speech factors:** "Stutters, mumbles, slurs [a negative attribute] . . . appropriate volume [and pitch] . . . speaks clearly . . . speaks at an appropriate pace . . . says 'um' or 'ah' [a negative attribute]" (p. 216)

Wood's (1998) extensive study reveals aspects of teacher behaviors that can help us in our teaching. For example, when we maintain good eye contact with our students, students' recall of the lecture is increased and their behavior in following instructions improves. Eye contact can produce a sense of personal connection between the professor and the students, "which can also encourage students to work harder" (Wood, 1998, p. 25).

In addition, the study found that humorous examples helped students recall material, but only when it was presented with nonhumorous material. Too many jokes are not effective; professors should limit their humor to a maximum of "four jokes per lecture" (Wood, 1998, p. 6). Berk (2002) also discusses the benefits of professors using humor in their lectures. He notes that humor can be used to build connections between the professor and his or her students, and it can immediately engage the students in "the learning process" (p. 4). Humor can also have an impact on one's classroom atmosphere or climate. As Berk points out,

> One of humor's most significant benefits is to create a relaxed, fun, and playful, but also intellectually stimulating environment conducive to learning. This is accomplished by its anxiety, tension, and stress reduction effects on just about everyone in the classroom—professor and students alike. (p. 60)

Although there are several benefits for using humor in our lectures, we also should be aware of a possible pitfall. If we use idioms that are culture specific in our jokes, the students who do not understand the joke because of the specific language usage can feel isolated or left out. This can have an unintentional negative effect in our classes.

Another suggestion for making our lectures effective is that we move around the room. Movement is important when we are talking, but it is also critical during class activity time. The purpose of our movements is to ensure we "will encounter a greater percentage of students. Students may be more likely to listen to a lecturer who is right in front of them compared to a lecturer who remains at a distance" (Wood, 1998, p. 21). During class activity time, students also stay on task when the professor moves around the room and checks in on groups.

Other critical aspects of effective lectures include speaking at an appropriate pace, not speaking in a monotone voice, and never reading verbatim from notes (Wood, 1998). When we show a strong interest in the subject and have appropriate facial expressions, most students respond favorably. For example, "a teacher's smile, gaze, nod of the head, and movement about the room may serve to reinforce student engagement in the lecture" (Wood, 1998, p. 25).

The overall results of Wood's (1998) study suggested that teacher enthusiasm "produces significant effects on student motivation, student attention, and student memory encoding" (p. 154). However, the study also found that "high levels of teacher enthusiasm are not enough to guarantee learning. In order to have a significant effect on learning, enthusiastic teaching behaviors must be strategic and coincide with the topic structure of a lecture" (p. 154). For example, having clarity of speech and being able to plan when to emphasize key points by slowing down, pausing, and changing pitch or volume can make a difference in student attention and recall. Although the teacher behaviors previously listed (clarity, enthusiasm, pacing, organization, and speech) contribute to students' views of their professors' enthusiasm, these alone will not help students' learning if there is not a clear structure to how the lecture is organized.

The results of Wood's study clearly demonstrate that teaching is not just a "song and dance," as some have suggested. Instead, instructors should determine the structure of their lectures ahead of time and then use the previously described enthusiastic teaching behaviors to increase student learning. Braxton (2008) also points out that "teaching skills that contribute to student course learning include organization and preparation, and instructional clarity . . . . These teaching skills also play a role in college student retention" (p. 104). Hence, the way we teach impacts not only our students' learning and learning experience, but also their success and ultimate graduation, especially for academically unprepared students, those from low-income family backgrounds, and those who traditionally have not been successful in finishing college.

Another technique that is beneficial is to outline the day's agenda on the board, in a PowerPoint slide, or on a handout at the beginning of class.

However, rather than just list a general outline, it is important to include critical concepts or principles that will be covered during the class period. Ambrose and colleagues (2010) note the following: "It is especially beneficial to help students create a useful organization as they are learning. To this end, providing an outline, agenda, or visual representation of each lecture, lab, or discussion session can give students a framework for organizing the information they are about to learn" (p. 61).

Then, when delivering the lecture, students are better able to follow along and take notes when subtopics are explicit, and we should also let them know when we are moving from one subtopic to another. It is also helpful to have the students use the class textbook during part of a lecture and/or during a class activity. Students can turn to the appropriate pages and connect the assigned reading to what's being covered in class. One example is to ask everyone in the class to turn to a page or section of the text that goes with the material that you are discussing in class.

We can also help students use their textbook by asking them (in pairs or groups of three) to answer probing questions regarding charts or illustrations on a particular page of their textbook. Furthermore, we can ask students to respond to additional or specialized information that is often in a special section of a textbook. I often give students a few minutes to discuss the information in the text with a partner before randomly calling on students to respond. When presenting additional information in a lecture, students can also compare the lecture information to what the author of the textbook has written.

PowerPoints, Class Notes, and Handouts

To accompany the lecture, most professors prepare a PowerPoint for each class meeting; in fact, the PowerPoint is a major tool that students expect to see as part of their professors' teaching. "Presenting with slides is so much a part of our culture now that people can hardly imagine preparing for a meeting [or class] . . . without slides" (Reynolds, 2008, p. 11). However, although PowerPoint is a technology tool that is intended to enrich, reinforce, and/or complement a lecture (and not repeat it), that is often not the case.

Many of the PowerPoints that professors prepare have slides that "are so jam-packed with graphs and figures that the fine print is difficult to read" (Kolowich, 2014, p. 8). Poorly constructed PowerPoints can frustrate students and interfere with their learning. On one hand, if a PowerPoint has too much information on each slide, the presentation can become tedious and boring, especially if the presenter reads the slides. On the other hand, PowerPoint presentations can contribute to students' acquisition of information if we apply some basic ground rules when making a PowerPoint. Reynolds (2008) notes that the PowerPoint "is not a method; it is a tool that can be used effectively with appropriate design methods, or ineffectively with inappropriate methods" (p. 12).

The first rule that Seth Godin, PowerPoint guru and presenter, states is this: "Make slides that reinforce your words, not repeat them" (Godin in Reynolds, 2008, p. 20). Thus, finding images that represent the subject matter is very effective. He provides this example: "Talking about pollution in Houston? Instead of giving me four bullet points of EPA data, why not read me the stats but show me a photo of a bunch of dead birds, some smog, and even a diseased lung?" (Godin in Reynolds, 2008, p. 20).

Orlando (2013) agrees and also recommends not using bullet points at all. He notes, "The real purpose of visuals is to amplify your message with complementary imagery . . . . The image does not compete with your audience's attention, but rather helps draw it together by providing a visual cue to enhance thinking" (p. 1). However, others note that two or three bullet points are okay, but only if phrases are used, not complete sentences, and if images are also added in subsequent slides.

Buchholz and Ullman (2004) recommend that only major ideas be put on a slide and details given orally. This avoids putting too much text on a slide. Slides simply should not be complicated with too many figures and tables. "If a large table needs to be part of a presentation, break it into chunks on several slides and focus on one aspect of it at a time" (Buchholz & Ullman, p. 4).[2] Other simple suggestions from Buchholz and Ullman and from Reynolds (2008) include the following:

1. Do not use busy backgrounds or colors that are ineffective; think contrast—colors should contrast (e.g., dark words on a light background or light words on a dark background).
2. Use animation or sounds in moderation; transitions should not be spinning or dissolving—keep it simple.
3. Use repetition of the slide design; "reusing the same or similar elements throughout . . . will bring a clear sense of unity, consistency, and cohesiveness" (p. 155).

The takeaway is that PowerPoints should support your lecture—not overtake your lecture. Face your students and talk to them with good eye contact. I also recommend using short video clips (less than three to no more than five minutes) with PowerPoints. The clip can be embedded in the PowerPoint, or you can switch to the video and then return to the PowerPoint. Finding appropriate video clips that relate to the topic or represent a dramatic or humorous example of what is being presented can be very effective, especially when followed with a Write-Pair-Share activity.

Professors should also emphasize that when lecturing (with or without PowerPoint slides) students should still take notes, and handwritten notes are most effective (Aguilar-Roca, Williams, & O'Dowd, 2012; Mueller & Oppenheimer, 2014). Cornelius and Owen-DeSchryver (2008) found that during lectures "[during] the process of taking notes, students gain some mastery of the material" (p. 11). Furthermore, they compared student-learning results in three different situations: students receiving a full set of notes, students receiving a partial set of notes in a handout, and students receiving no notes or handouts.

Cornelius and Owen-DeSchryver (2008) also found that providing a full set of notes to the students has an adverse effect. Furthermore, giving no notes or even partial notes also had a negative effect. In contrast, giving a handout with a partial set of instructor notes or a brief outline was found to be helpful. It is important to emphasize to the students that they need to learn how use their own words when taking class notes.

> If the intent of college teaching is to help students master the material and facilitate higher level learning, then providing full notes appears to be inhibiting these processes. Partial notes, therefore, may provide a nice balance in terms of providing students with some notes, which they report as helpful, and still requiring encoding and higher level processing of information, which will ultimately improve learning and performance. (Cornelius & Owen-DeSchryver, 2008, p. 11)

Thus, even if students are poor notetakers, which many freshmen are (not just unprepared students), they need to begin practicing taking notes right away so that as they go through the semester their note-taking skills will improve.

We can also assist students by giving them tips on how to improve their note-taking skills (see Appendix D) as well as signaling to them key points that need to be written down during the first few lectures of the semester. Signals can be as obvious as "This is important, so write it down" or "There are three key important points—first . . . second . . . etc." Another helpful practice is for us to pause for a few minutes during a lecture and ask students to look over their notes and add reflections on what has been covered so far.

Conclusion

As we have seen, although the practice of giving traditional lectures is still common at colleges and universities, it is not always the best way to foster learning and indeed has disadvantages for minority, first-generation, and academically unprepared students. Astin (1999b) implores us, the professors, to "design more effective learning environments" (p. 518). As the professors in charge of our courses, we can strive to design learning environments where there is an equal educational opportunity for our diverse student body, not just the fewer high-achieving students who can process a nonstop 50-minute lecture.

Braxton (2006) believes that, as professors, we can make "professional choices in teaching that foster student success" (p. 107). One important choice is to incorporate interactive lectures with meaningful educational activities. In doing so, we can have a significant impact on our students' view of their capabilities as well as their perceptions about lifelong learning. It is in our classrooms where we can create pathways to success that will support the retention, persistence, and eventual graduation of all students, and especially our historically underrepresented and underserved students.

Furthermore, college and university administrators can help by supporting and encouraging professors to expend effort incorporating learning-centered teaching methods (e.g., interactive lectures) by awarding "tenure, promotion, continued appointment, and increases in annual salary" (Braxton, 2008, p. 107). After all, "faculty use of active learning practices directly and indirectly affects college student departure decisions" (Braxton, Jones, Hirschy, & Hartley, 2008, p. 72). Professors have many demands on their time, but teaching our students is of utmost importance. Our students deserve our attention and time. Indeed, teaching should be at the top of colleges' and universities' priority list—not the bottom.

Notes

1. Lectures are often viewed as the only way to teach a large class of 70 to 100 students and super large classes of 150 to 500 or more students gathered in a single lecture hall.

2. All references need to be posted on the PowerPoint, and the same rules for plagiarism and citing sources that are in writing apply when writing in a PowerPoint.

6

READING ASSIGNMENTS
AND CLASS DISCUSSIONS

Stimulate Deeper Learning

Reading furnishes the mind only with materials of knowledge;
it is thinking that makes what we read ours.

—John Locke (1632–1704)

Introduction

Reading assignments of textbooks, journal articles, and novels are ubiquitous in the college and university landscape. Despite listing the "required texts" on the syllabus, many of us who are "teaching faculty" often are concerned students will not complete the required readings and may not even buy (or rent) the required texts. How can this be? Perhaps students do not grasp the value and necessity of the assigned reading, or is it more? Bean (2001) notes, "Many students are poor readers, overwhelmed by the density of their college textbooks and baffled by the strangeness and complexity of primary sources and by their unfamiliarity with academic discourse" (p. 133).

This problem is not new; it cannot be ignored, nor should it be side-stepped. Reading is an essential learning activity for college and university courses. "If high levels of student reading compliance and, by extension, high levels of reading comprehension, are endpoints that truly matter, faculty must accept their role in an inter-dependent process; they are the key agents in making reading fundamental in college" (Hobson, n.d., p. 8).

Requiring textbooks (or other reading materials) and spelling out students' responsibility for acquiring texts are only the first two parts of our role. Equally important, many believe that, as professors, we need to ensure that our students know how to read and use textbooks, other types of books, and readings (e.g., journals) in an effective way to expand their own knowledge. Students also need to understand the purpose of readings to stimulate deeper learning and critical thinking, as well as broaden horizons and expand worldviews. In today's world of the Internet, social media, and "fake" news, it is crucial that our students be able to identify and evaluate all kinds of sources as well as the quality of those sources. The purpose of this chapter is to explore several ways we can encourage our students to read and help them become critical and reflective thinkers.

Required Books: "Choose 'Em and Use 'Em"

When Astin (1999b) describes engagement that is necessary for success in college, he clarifies that it is not just the number of hours (a quantitative measure) that is imperative, but also the type of studying that takes place (qualitative features). For example, we need to consider "whether the student reviews and comprehends reading assignments or simply stares at the textbook and daydreams" (Astin, 1999b, p. 519). However, before either can happen, the students must obtain the required books. There are steps that we, as professors, can take to increase the chances that everyone will have the required texts for in-class and out-of-class use.

First, when picking out a textbook, consider the cost. Professors at most institutions are vigilant in seeking out reasonably priced texts. If the most appropriate textbook is one that is "bundled" with a compact disc (CD) and study guide, and if the CD or study guide is not being used, then we can request to have it "unbundled" so that the textbook can be purchased for less. We also can use the same book for as many semesters as possible so that students can take advantage of buying the lesser priced used books.

Second, we can allow students to buy an earlier edition of the text. This can result in huge savings; for example, an earlier edition might cost less than $50 compared to $100 for the latest edition. For one of my classes, the textbook of the earlier edition was approximately $35 compared to the newest version for $110. Regarding new and pertinent information in the latest edition, as professors we can usually supplement the earlier edition through class lectures and/or handouts.

Third, many low-income, first-generation, and other students are relying on student loans, and if their loans or financial aid has not arrived as the semester begins, they will put off buying books. To make sure the students have access to the books for my courses, I have acquired extra books (at least 1 or 2 per course) and have these books on "reserve" in the college library with a 24-hour checkout so that a student cannot dominate the text on reserve; with a 24-hour checkout, a student can take the book home for a day. In addition, at many institutions, we can put in a "purchase request" to the college librarian so that our texts will be available for regular checkout. That way, students who are waiting for financial aid can check out the book from the library.[1]

In addition to the cost, Nilson (n.d.) suggests that we consider the average reading ability of the students at our college or university and look at the types of illustrations and graphics our books have to reinforce the material. Of course, above all considerations, in order for texts to be central to the course success, they must be course related and relevant. After books are selected, it is important to explain to the students why the texts were chosen "as well as their purpose, value, and relevance to the course" (Nilson, n.d., p. 1).

These suggestions can be crucial as we seek ways to ensure that our students will buy and then read the textbook we choose for our courses, but doing them still will not guarantee that all students will purchase the required books. The syllabus should expressly state that the books are required, but that also will not ensure that all the students will obtain them. One problem is that students may have had other courses where the so-called required textbooks were not used or needed in class, for assignments or for exams. In these cases, students have often succeeded without reading, especially if instructors presented the important information in class (Doyle, 2008; Leamnson, 1999). Hence, many students may not really believe us when we tell them that our books are required.

At some point, a professor may feel a little weary of dealing with the textbook drama (costs, students not reading or buying the books) and tell students that the textbook is optional. McGuire (2015) warns us that this is not conducive for student learning, especially for at-risk or struggling students. She implores all professors to require students to obtain the textbooks for their courses and not allow students to rely only on lecture notes. As students are learning and mastering complex material, they need the textbook to help them fill in the blanks and support what was covered in class. She explains:

> When we as instructors read the lecture notes, our minds fill in everything that is missing, so everything does genuinely appear to be there. If you are among those who tell your students that they do not need to buy the book, I know you are not deliberately sabotaging them and that you are just trying to save them money. But their minds are not your minds. They need the textbook. (McGuire, 2015, p. 50)

Weimer (2010) agrees that we should not just give in and stop asking students to purchase textbooks or read them. She advises, "We can't just bemoan the fact that students don't read . . . . *The better solution involves designing courses so that students can't do well without reading* . . . . The assignments must be structured so that students engage and respond to the reading" (p. 6; emphasis added).

As professors, one way we can hold students accountable is to require them to bring the textbook(s) to every single class meeting and then use it during class activities or during the lecture at least once or twice per class. Boyd (n.d.) uses this policy in her classes, as do I. She reports that many first-year students in beginning classes do not realize the importance of having the book, and older students want assurances that the book will actually be used. (Also see chapter 5 for additional ways to use the textbook during class.)

Students can be reassured if we take the time to introduce the text. We can show them how the text is organized, what its key features are, and information about the author(s) (discussed in greater detail later in the chapter; Culver & Morse, 2008). Nilson (n.d.) points out that students see these explanations as a sign of "respect" (p. 1) and also recommends the following: "At the first class meeting, tell them [the students] that they will have to read and possibly even mark up the books daily for a chance at a passing final grade. If they can't or won't buy the books, they should drop your course" (p. 1). If we adopt a "must have the textbook" policy, then accountability and follow-up are essential (i.e., having a consequence for students who do not have the book in class). Because I use class activity points (similar to class participation points) as part of the course grade, any student who does not have the textbook in class cannot earn full class activity points. I give the students a grace period to obtain the book: the first two class meetings. By the third class, class activity points are affected. Thus, I have found that students always bring the book to class.

During the first two classes, I find it extremely beneficial to move around the room as students are completing a class activity and record the names of anyone who does not have a textbook. I will ask each student without a book to stay after class or make an appointment to see me before the next class. (For larger classes, I cannot always get to every group, so it might take two classes to get around to everyone.)

As I meet with each student individually, I don't just ask the student why he or she doesn't have the book in class, but also ask, "How can I help?" With this kind of follow-up, students will know that we are sincere about upholding our book policy. With the one-on-one meetings, we also have a chance to build rapport with our students and discuss the benefits of having the textbook. Once we assure our students that the book will be used during every class meeting, we can also explain how the book will help them prepare for the exams. Knowing that the textbook will be used is a relief to many students, and many have shared with me their frustration over spending a lot of money on a textbook only to find out that it was never used in class or for exams.

As mentioned previously, another successful strategy for getting students to buy the required textbook is to refer to it throughout the class period. When students know we will be connecting our lectures and class activities to the text(s), the value of having the text in class becomes obvious. Weimer (2002) models textbook use for her students during class. She explains, "I bring my book to class and try to use it in ways that demonstrate and underscore what it contributes to our efforts to learn course content" (p. 105). She also has consequences for students if they have not done the reading. By holding students accountable for their actions, "students will start assuming more responsibility for their learning" (p. 106).

Even though the textbook is used in class, Fink (2013) recommends not trying to cover or summarize *all* the readings. Doing so is a clear signal to students that they do not have to read and can just get what they need from the lecture (Fink, 2013). This has been referred to as the "just wait for the movie" syndrome. It is helpful to let students know that they are responsible for assigned readings and that there will not be lectures in class detailing or summarizing key points of the reading assignments. Equally important is follow-up, and this can be accomplished by "testing students as thoroughly on required reading material [as on material covered in class]" (Boyd, n.d., p. 2). Testing can come in several forms, such as traditional exams, quizzes, and writing reflections.

In addition to choosing an appropriate textbook and using it in class, we need to consider supplementing the textbook with additional readings if the textbook has a mainly Eurocentric perspective and/or does not include information about multicultural issues or people in the field who are minorities and women. As discussed in chapters 2 and 3, it can be beneficial for all our students when we create an inclusive classroom and incorporate culturally relevant material into our course's traditional content, if it is not already there. Including readings that address multicultural topics or that are written by minority authors is one way we can expose all our students to world or global views beyond the Eurocentric perspective. As professors, we can look for ways to do this for every single course we teach.

When we include culturally relevant readings, the message can speak to everyone in our class in an inclusive way. Shetterly (2016) responded to questions about her book, *Hidden Figures: The American Dream and the Untold Story of the Black Women Mathematicians Who Helped Win the Space Race*, by saying the following:

> There's something about this story that seems to resonate with people of all races, ethnicities, genders, ages, and backgrounds. It's a story of hope, that even among some of our country's harshest realities—legalized segregation,

racial discrimination—there is evidence of the triumph of meritocracy, that each of us should be allowed to rise as far as our talent and hard work can take us. (p. 247)

By including multicultural readings that will be used in class activities and discussions, we can promote connectedness and bring a sense of belonging to everyone in our classroom (Johnson et al., 2007). Rendon (2006) points out that when referring to student retention and success, we should include "the extent that the student develops a worldview, appreciates difference, [and] becomes a critical/reflective thinker" (p. 8). As students remain in school to fulfill their course of study, the more they also learn about "differences [and similarities] between people and cultures, the more effective they will be in all parts of their lives" (Heuberger, Gerber, & Anderson, 1999, p. 107).

Preparing for Class: Reflections and Responses

Once students bring their books to class, the next challenge is getting them to actually complete the reading assignments before class. One way to encourage students to do this is to design class activities where students are using information from the text. Thus, if students have not completed the reading assignment before class, it hampers their performance; however, by having their books in class, students are not completely "washed out" if they did not prepare for class. (See chapter 5 for further discussion on interactive lectures.) Once students realize how the reading will help them in class, most will make changes in how they prepare for class.

Conducting learning tasks that require the use of the textbook during class will assist students in learning how to use and read the text on their own. When students delve into the text, they usually generate questions and discussions about the reading. This, in turn, can help them learn how to read more effectively on their own. For example, activities that promote a deeper level of learning can include "paraphrasing or summarizing the material to be learned, creating analogies, [and] generative note-taking (where the student actually re-organizes and connects ideas in their notes)" (Pintrich, 1999, p. 460). To do these activities in class, students need to have their books and notes with them. (See later in this chapter and chapter 7 for further discussion and specific examples.)

One class activity that promotes reading before class and using the text during class is from Barkley (2009), where students respond to quotes that the professor has selected. This activity provides equal participation by providing "all students with a platform by which to join the discussion. It also underscores the instructor's commitment to the value of the assigned reading" (p. 267). When students realize that they will have to speak specifically about some aspect of the reading to their classmates, their motivation to get the reading done before class is increased. Barkley gives step-by-step directions for setting up the activity:

1. Select 5–6 different sentences or passages from a text.
2. Type and copy these to create multiple slips of paper each containing one quote, and put them into a container.
3. Each student draws one slip of paper.
4. Students take a few minutes to think about what they want to say in response to their quote.
5. In an order controlled by students, the discussion continues with each student reading a quote and commenting on it, offering new insight or building upon or contradicting comments that already have been made. (p. 167)

I found keeping the group size to only four students to be the most effective. I also made a few minor adjustments when using this activity. The first adjustment is that I have the students in each group draw only one quote at a time, and after the first student reads his or her quote and others comment, then the next student takes his or her turn. A second adjustment is that all students are required to have their books out and each must turn to the page where the quote that is being read and discussed is found.

Next, I fold up the slips of paper and put them in a small bowl with a lid or a small ziplock type of plastic bag. At the end of the activity, all the slips of paper are returned to the container and given back to me so I can use them again for another section of the class or for the following semester. Thus, for a class of 48 students, 12 ziplock bags are prepared; for smaller classes of 28 students, I use 8 small plastic bowls. For classes with uneven numbers, there may be a group with only 3 students.

My students enjoy this activity immensely. The first time I use the activity in a class, I put 4 quotes in the bag so everyone gets only one turn, and it takes about 10 minutes to complete. However, the second time I have the class do this activity, I use 8 quotes, and schedule more time. Everyone in each group now has two turns. Barkley (2009) notes, "The time required will depend on the nature, scope and complexity of the quotes and the reading assignment from which they were taken" (p. 169). Finally, Barkley recommends that we move around the room and listen in on several of the groups' discussions.

A second constructive activity that promotes being prepared for class is to assign a reading reflection/response to be turned in (on hard copy typed double-spaced in 12-point font) the day that the reading assignment is due. I have students keep their papers until we have had a class discussion so that they can refer back to what they have written. The requirement of having a typed "hard" copy also prevents anyone from attempting to complete the homework during class. I assign such reflections periodically throughout the semester and provide questions that students must respond to. I give them guidelines on how to prepare their short reading reflection/response, including use of quotes and length.

For larger classes, I limit their responses to 1 page; for smaller upper division classes, the reflections can be longer but no more than 2 pages (typed double-spaced). I also require students to include 1 or 2 quotes but no more (with a total of no more than 40 words quoted) to be part of their reflection (or response) so that they have to refer back to a specific part of the reading. Students have their books and response papers in hand as they participate in a class activity, be it a pair-share or a small-group discussion.

Weir (2009) also uses this strategy to ensure reading. He states, "If you want students to read, make it hard (or impossible) to avoid" (p. 1). His assignment is a little different from mine but a similar idea. It is also a great example of how this technique can be varied to fit different professors' goals and teaching situations. Weir describes his assignment briefly:

> These need not be elaborate . . . . I require periodic two- to three-page papers for most reading assignments. Four or five questions appear on the course Web site and students must write about one of them . . . . It also allows me to monitor student writing and gives me clues about what I must address before a major assignment comes along. (p. 1)

I find it helpful not to accept late papers because the point of the assignment is to get students to be "prepared" for class. Also, by keeping the points (grade value) for each paper fairly low, it can make it easier to give this kind of assignment several times during the semester, and with feedback, students can have plenty of opportunities to improve. (See chapter 7 for further discussion on writing assignments.) Although I keep the response/reflection paper short, students are still required to "grapple" with the assigned readings and not just summarize key points. We can help students do that in the kind of questions or prompts we give them.

A third technique many professors have found effective is to take the last five minutes of the previous class to give an overview of the assigned reading due for the next class (or classes). Depending on how many times the class meets during a week, the overview might be for the next few classes (e.g., at Friday's class giving students an overview for the following classes on

Monday, Wednesday, and Friday). The purpose in doing this is threefold: (a) to attempt to get students excited about the reading, (b) to point out the relevance of the reading, and (c) to highlight for the students key points to look for as they read.

One way to build excitement for the upcoming reading assignment is to propose a problem, mystery, or scenario that arouses curiosity. It can even be presented in a video clip. Then, advise the students that they will find possible solutions or answers in the week's reading. The Office of Support for Effective Teaching (2009) at the University of New Mexico advises professors to guide students by letting them know what is important and/or what they should learn from the reading before they come to class.

I witnessed a science professor use this technique by showing a clip from the film *Erin Brockovich*. The clip showed one of the early scenes where she is investigating the cause of the devastating illnesses of residents in a local community. After showing the less than two-minute video clip, the professor gave questions to the students to consider as they read their next assignment, which covered the Centers for Disease Control and Prevention and how investigations are handled. Needless to say, the students' interest was definitely sparked. Although providing this type of overview may not be practical with every assignment, it can be fun to figure out ways to arouse students' curiosity and interest in the reading and increase the likelihood that students will complete the reading assignment (Bean, 2001; Davis, 1993).

We can also increase students' interest in the reading assignments by pointing out the relevancy of the reading. According to Hobson (n.d.), "Making the implicit explicit helps those students who need the most assistance in reading and comprehending course materials, particularly marginally skilled and unskilled readers" (p. 5). Along with explaining the relevancy, introducing the next reading assignment gives students guidance as to what key points they will be learning about from the reading. There are classes where the assignment has to be turned in, but I remind the students to still take reading notes—either directly in the book (as margin notes) or separately on paper. Student should be aware that

> just as writing promotes active listening in class, writing also promotes active reading outside of class. Recording [writing] notes on what is being read while it is being read ensures active involvement, because it involves more mental and physical energy than merely reading the material, or passively underlining sentences with a magic marker. (Cuseo, 2010, p. 2)

To add accountability, the day that the reading is to be done, we can ask students to write "short" answers to a few questions that are displayed on the overhead projector, a document camera, a visual projector, or a PowerPoint slide. Some professors will put up more questions (three or four) and give the students a choice of answering only one or two. When using this method, I allow students to use their notes and book, and it takes about five minutes.

Doing this for every class may not be feasible, nor is it necessary to assign reading reflections (as described previously) for every class. However, by always having a set of readings that go with the topic covered, Coffman (2009) points out that "using the book in class helps to establish its importance" (p. 15). Furthermore, by pointing out to the students the current assigned reading pages or the following week's pages due, students are "more likely to read" than if the reading is just listed on the syllabus calendar (Hobson, n.d.).

Anticipating Difficulty With the Reading: Five Steps to Use

When it comes to the reading and math skills of high school graduates, "The American College Testing Program (2005) declared that the nation has 'a college readiness crisis'" (Kuh, Kinzie, Buckley, Bridges, & Hayek, 2006, p. 2). Because many students have been able to get by in high school without putting in much study time (less than six hours a week), they "appear to start college already 'disengaged' from the learning process, having acquired a cumulative deficit in terms of attitudes, study habits, and academic skills" (Kuh et al., 2006, p. 33).

It is hard to tell whether students are having difficulty with the reading assignments or just not putting in the time necessary to complete the reading. "One out of five college students self-report that they frequently come to class without completing the readings or other assignments that were expected to be completed before class (NSSE, 2008)" (Office of Support for Effective Teaching, 2009, p. 2). Part of college is learning how to self-regulate, self-monitor, and self-manage study or academic time. When they first come to college, many students, including those who are academically unprepared, "have no idea what it takes to succeed academically at the college level when they first begin. The amount of time and commitment that is demanded from them often comes as a shock" (Gabriel, 2008, p. 17). However, students can make changes, with our help and guidance.

First, as professors, we can have discussions with our students about our expectations of what they need to accomplish *outside* of class. Giving students a "time" or estimation of how many hours they will need to spend outside of class can be tricky because it can vary greatly. Still, we can be clear that when students read the textbook, diligence and effort will be needed.

Reading a chapter once or skimming it is not sufficient, even though this might have worked in high school (Culver & Morse, 2008). Furthermore, we can share with our students that heavy highlighting, even with multiple colors, is an unproductive practice for grasping the material. With a lot of highlighting, all the student has is a textbook with bright and colorful pages, not improved comprehension.

Second, as mentioned previously, introducing students to the textbook is something all students can benefit from, but as professors, we can also share insights into "how an expert reads . . . [to help students] anticipate the content of a particular reading" (Nilson, n.d., p. 2). Previewing the subheadings, illustrations, graphs, charts, and italicized words and reading the first and last paragraphs are ways for readers to recognize the "destination" and purpose of the chapter. Bean (2001) notes that many students think that expert readers are speed-readers, and will "push themselves to read faster instead of slower. Consequently, they do not allot enough study time for reading and rereading" (p. 134). Our students must understand that even excellent readers will read and reread difficult text, along with "writing gist statements in the margins" (Bean, 2001, p. 134).

Third, during short class lectures, we can have students turn to illustrations, graphs, tables, or charts in the book when reviewing them. (Also see chapter 5 for further discussion on using textbooks during class.) Boyd (n.d.) notes that when professors do this, if a student does not have the book, the discomfort alone motivates him or her to start bringing the book to class. To promote class preparation as well as having the book in class, I use "random calling" on students rather than asking students to raise their hand to respond because the ones who raise their hand are usually the ones who have done the reading. To spare students any embarrassment, for each class period, students are given one pass (one get-out-of-answering pass). This is how it can work: Call on someone, and he or she can answer the question or say, "I pass." Then respond in a way that lets the student know that it is okay to use the pass, such as, "That's fine, and that's your one pass for today." This can be helpful for students who are nervous about using the pass and at the same time lets them know they cannot use a pass throughout the class session. Next, call on someone else. If a student who is called on is clearly unprepared or pausing for a long period of time, remind him or her that the pass can be used but the choice is entirely up to the student.

To ensure that calling on students is random, Nilson (n.d.) recommends that you "put each of your students' name on an index card and shuffle the deck" (p. 3). After pulling a card, if the student takes a pass or gives an incorrect answer, you can make a mark on the card indicating a "good-faith 'grade,' [but then] return the card to the deck, and shuffle again. Don't let anyone feel too safe or get too comfortable!" (p. 3).

Fourth, students do better when they read with a purpose. For example, when students are seeking to answer study guide or guided-reading questions, reading comprehension improves. The questions might be ones that are in the textbook, or ones that have been created by the professor. We can help students with their reading by asking them to complete such guides. The guided-reading questions can also include problem-solving prompts.

Eddy and Hogan (2014) also found positive results when students were given guided-reading questions to use as they completed the readings outside of class. Even though the completed guides were not collected or graded, "these questions helped to teach active reading (beyond highlighting) and to reinforce practice study skills, such as drawing, using the content in each chapter" (p. 456). Furthermore, the process of figuring out the answers to the guided-reading questions assisted the students as they participated in class activities and in their test preparation and performance.

Finally, the fifth step for addressing difficulties in reading is to consider students' reading comprehension skills. Bean (2001) notes, "Inadequate vocabulary hampers the reading comprehension of many students" (p. 136). Students need to be challenged, but "if the academic work is too challenging and beyond what a person can do, then the student might miss the point of its relevancy and usefulness. Often reading assignments are too difficult for at-risk and unprepared students to comprehend" (Gabriel, 2008, p. 111).

One way to help students confront their reading challenges is by teaching them an effective strategy for improving their vocabulary (Appendix E provides an example of such a strategy). In all my teaching years, I have taught many students who had academic deficiencies when I first met them. Once these students were taught how to use evidence-based learning strategies, the vast majority were able to make significant improvements by putting in time and effort to learn and apply the strategies. We can help our students, but above all they "must accept responsibility for learning" (Weimer, 2002, p. 95).

Another way to help students confront reading challenges is to encourage students to monitor their own comprehension by tackling words that they do not know, instead of just skipping over them. By doing this, students will be taking a step in the right direction. I advise students to use the dictionary profusely and make flash cards following the vocabulary strategy outlined in Appendix E. This vocabulary strategy can be taught in a class or during office hours, review, or even tutoring sessions. To continue to help their learning, students must continually self-assess and self-test until new words are mastered.

Reading and Critical Thinking Skills

Laird, Chen, and Kuh (2008) note that academic challenge "includes the amount of reading and writing students do for their courses, [and] the amount of emphasis their courses place on higher order thinking skills such as analysis and synthesis" (p. 89). In order for students to use the higher order thinking skills, we can structure our courses so that we are emphasizing deeper approaches to learning, but also providing students "with the necessary support when they encounter problems" (Laird et al., 2008, p. 95).

Critical thinking, a higher order thinking skill, has been defined in several ways. Halpern (2012) notes that "it is purposeful, reasoned, and goal directed. It is the kind of thinking involved in solving problems, formulating inferences, calculating likelihoods, and making decisions" (p. 2). Nilson (2014) adds "that critical thinking entails an interpretation or analysis, usually followed by evaluation or judgment . . . . It means learners must be willing to pursue 'truth' to wherever it may lie" (p. 1). Sharing definitions of critical thinking is one way to help our students recognize the challenges we are giving them. Their task is not to memorize facts and ideas, but "to weigh evidence and evaluate facts and ideas critically" (Braxton, 2006, p. 4). We can assist our students in tackling these different aspects of critical thinking by formulating questions "that require students to respond thoughtfully to a text and then to build these into the course as part of a reading guide" (Bean, 2001, p. 145).

Paul, Elder, and Bartell (2015) add that critical thinking includes a "recognition that all reasoning occurs within points of view and frames of reference" (p. 4). An exercise that we can have our students do to practice critical thinking is to have them investigate the author(s) of the required textbook and other assigned reading. Bean (2001) points out that students' interests can be sparked when we introduce them to the author's background and share how the author can bring his or her "own selectivity, emphasis, and writing style" (p. 140). Students can investigate views of the subject "from competing textbooks or other scholarly works and . . . explore the differences between them" (Bean, 2001, p. 140). Students will read more actively when they are looking for a point of view, or evaluating the author's point of view and frame of reference.

While Culver and Morse (2008) recommend that we refer to the textbook in class when giving short lectures so that students can make clear connections to the text, they also suggest that we let the students know whether we are presenting a different view. They state, "Make it clear to the students why and how [our] position differs" (Culver & Morse, 2008, p. 7). Additionally, when presenting a different view (along with sources), we can have students discuss (or debate) the different arguments. As students are seeking to evaluate material, make inferences, or solve problems, it is equally important for them to be able to figure out where the information came from and what kind of research is backing (or not backing) the claims.

We often hear students (and others) use the phrase "research shows . . ." followed by the sharing of information. However, the details of the actual research, such as the author(s), the methods used for the study, and the number of people in the study, are usually omitted. Likewise, students are continually using the Internet to gather information but often do not look for the source, the author(s), the organization that is sponsoring the web page, and so on. Many do not know how to do this, and it may not even occur to them that it should be done. By asking for the "details" of the research or information being presented, we can increase students' awareness and assessment skills.

Additionally, when asking students to read academic research articles, be it for a paper or just additional content for your course, going over the structure of these kinds of readings can be helpful. Laubepin (2013) has outlined an excellent procedure for students, titled "How to Read (and Understand) a Social Science Journal Article." Another handout that also gives students simple and straightforward information for reading research articles is titled "How to Read a Research Study Article" (Franzoi & Ratlif-Crain, 2003). I have used both handouts and found them to be very helpful, especially for many of the students who had little experience in reading any kinds of peer-reviewed journal articles.

Halpern (2012) suggests that we can help our students develop a critical thinking approach to the things they see and hear in the media, including radio, music, magazines, and television. However, we must emphasize to students that it is important to know who (or what group) is financing or supporting a particular website, and what is the bias or point of view the author(s) support. As students, and as citizens of a democracy, they need to learn how to investigate the authors and sources of any material they are reading. (For further discussion on evaluating sources see chapter 7.) Teaching students how to read using critical thinking skills, including how to fact-check, will provide our students with tools they can use for life.

Another strategy for advancing critical thinking of reading assignments is to assign "reading" roles to each member of the small discussion groups. To help the students fulfill their roles, Reeves-Cohen (2003) suggests five specific roles along with descriptions of each role:

1. Facilitator—creates discussion questions, monitors flow of discussion. Should come to class prepared with three discussion questions to which

the group will respond in discussion. Questions should refer to a specific part of the text and be open-ended to promote discussion.

2. Jargon scout—chooses a new or provocative word[s] from the text, defines it, and discusses usage. Should come to class prepared with the word[s] . . . definition, a quotation from the text in which it is used, and the student's own example of a possible usage. [Professors can ask the jargon scout to bring three or four words.]

3. Contextualizer—chooses a passage or idea from the text that has a personal connection or refers to another area of study. Should come to class prepared with the passage and a description of the connection he/she discovers. How are the two ideas/events related? Does their connection change the way you might look at the two separately?

4. Close reader—picks a passage that is particularly challenging and presents it with questions for analysis. Should come to class prepared with the passage under consideration and a series of questions/comments that the group will discuss in order to clarify.

5. Devil's advocate—identifies the primary argument or assumption of the reading (or the discussion) and argues an alternative viewpoint. Should come to class prepared with a summary of the primary thrust of the reading and at least one other possible viewpoint with supporting information.

Once students are assigned a role, they are asked to prepare for their roles, type their preparation notes, and bring two copies to class—one to turn in to the professor and one to keep for notes and use in their small-group discussions. Reeves-Cohen (2003) also suggests that students do not keep the same role if this activity is used more than once, but alternate their roles and groups.

Other types of reading activities that will promote students' critical thinking are "paraphrasing or summarizing the material to be learned, creating analogies, [and] generative note-taking (where the student actually reorganizes and connects ideas in their notes)" (Pintrich, 1999, p. 460). Bean (2001) suggests the following questions to which we might have students respond:

What confused you in today's class or today's reading?
How does your own personal experience relate to what you studied today?
What effect is this course having on your personal life, your beliefs, your values, your precious understanding of things?
How does what we have been studying recently relate to your other courses or to other parts of this course? (p. 107)

There are different ways to have students interact with the reading to promote individual responsibility, encourage collaborative learning, and support the class atmosphere of having a *community of learners.* By having support from fellow students and the professor, students can face academic challenges and advance their critical thinking skills.

Conclusion

Hobson (n.d.) notes that "a commitment to reading is one of the essential tools necessary for higher order thought, rational action, and fulfillment" (p. 8). How we handle the selections of texts and how those texts are used in our classes are paramount to students' learning and success. Using approaches that will help students address their reading difficulties should not be disregarded; indeed, to close the graduation gap, we can make teaching choices that assist students who are struggling when they first start college.

Getting students to read is only part of our teaching challenge. In addition, we can facilitate student improvement and growth in their levels of comprehension, analysis, application, and evaluation—all critical thinking skills that are a vital part of how we use reading assignments for our classes. Being able to identify sources and investigate authors is another critical component of improving reading (and thinking) skills.

To assist students in reaching higher and deeper learning levels, the "process . . . takes time, during which direct instruction and continuous modeling by faculty members and student maturation must occur" (Hobson, n.d., p. 8). Above all, when students have positive experiences with reading, their disposition for reading can become a lifelong habit. *Lifelong learning* can be defined "as a love of learning that manifests itself in a continuation of intellectual interests after leaving college and which includes a knowledge of how to learn" (Braxton, 2006, p. 4). Proper handling of reading assignments and follow-up activities in our colleges and universities will inspire our students to continue reading throughout their adult lives.

Note

1. I do not allow electronic devices during class time, so my students are required to have a hard copy in class; because ebooks or books on a computer (or smartphone) are not allowed in my class, having books in the library for checkout is very important.

7

WRITING ASSIGNMENTS

Promote Critical Thinking and Writing

The most important attitude that can be formed is that of desire to go on learning.

—*John Dewey (1859–1952)*

Introduction

Many students begin college lacking the academic writing skills and experience that are required to succeed in college. In 2007, the National Assessment of Educational Progress reported that "77% of 12th-grade students did not meet . . . writing proficiency goals" (Graham & Perin, 2007, p. 8). For example, in high school, many students "were rarely required to criticize an argument, define a problem and propose a solution, shape their writing to meet their readers' needs, or revise based on feedback" (Eberly Center, 2008). Writing a term paper (can also be called a capstone or research paper) longer than six or seven pages with academic sources or references is another experience many students have not had before coming to college.

Miller (2009) notes that writing "is a complex form of communication that requires specific technical skills . . . as well as self-expression abilities" (p. 340). It is often thought that being a good reader will carry over to being a good writer. However, reading and writing skills do not always go hand in hand. Students can have average to above-average reading skills for their grade level and, at the same time, deficits in and difficulties with their writing skills (Graham & Perin, 2007). In contrast, improving writing skills does have a positive and effective impact on literacy skills, including reading comprehension (Gabriel & Davis, 2015; Graham & Perin, 2007).

The purpose of this chapter is to demonstrate how we can assign writing tasks in our courses in order to promote learning and engagement and also help students improve their writing skills and critical thinking. Additionally, I address how to deal with student procrastination for major writing projects, how to avoid plagiarism, and strategies we can use to help our students evaluate sources that they use when writing term or research papers.

The suggestions offered in this chapter are not meant to be a panacea for fixing students' writing skills. Weimer (2002) advises, "No one can do everything that needs to be done for learners . . . . Do not take it upon yourself to do everything that needs to be done with students" (p. 57). She reminds us that our campus's learning center has professionals and tutors who can be very important "partners" in our efforts to assist students. Nevertheless, as professors, we can have a positive impact on our students' writing skills, and in doing so, we can share with our students that "teaching writing is not just the 'job' of the English Department . . . . It is the responsibility of all faculty" (LEARN Center, 2017). Morales (2014) points out that when we consider "ethnic minorities and students from low socioeconomic demographics of the United States . . . [college faculty have] . . . the most influence over the potential success of these students" (p. 92). Thus, how we interact with our students and the feedback we give them on their writing can be of utmost importance for encouraging them to make improvements and not give up.

The Quintessential Value of the Written Word

Writing tasks are often a vital component of higher education and allow students to demonstrate their competence and knowledge of course material (e.g., lab reports, critiques, essay exams). In addition, for many courses, students must also integrate course concepts and content with outside sources (e.g., peer-reviewed journal articles) in a formal, structured writing project such as term or research papers. As professors, many of us also assign writing tasks to help our students become active learners and critical thinkers who "confront problems, gather and analyze data, prepare hypotheses, and formulate arguments" (Centre for Teaching Excellence, n.d.a). These are just some examples illuminating how writing tasks are a crucial part of college courses. Still, as professors, many of us are surprised and even frustrated with the low writing skills of most of our students, especially when these students are in their third or fourth year of college.

Nowacek (2011) describes the importance of writing for college courses and beyond, including professional careers and citizenship participation in everyday lives. Some of the benefits she lists for students are as follows:

- Writing is the primary basis upon which your work, your learning, and your intellect will be judged—in college, in the workplace, and in the community.
- Writing expresses who you are as a person.
- Writing is portable and permanent. It makes your thinking visible.

- Writing helps you move easily among facts, inferences, and opinions without getting confused—and without confusing your reader.
- Writing equips you with the communication and thinking skills you need to participate effectively in democracy.
- Writing is an essential job skill. (http://www.marquette.edu/wac/What-MakesWritingSoImportant.shtml)

Sharing this list with students can help make them aware of the significance of writing. Many students will put forth more attention, time, and effort in their writing assignments once they hear from us that we value writing. In addition, if appropriate, this can also be a time when professors can explain to the students that different disciplines have differing approaches to writing, and, therefore, you will be emphasizing certain criteria that fit your course and discipline.

There are many meaningful educational activities where writing exercises can be incorporated and, at the same time, promote active learning. Bonwell and Eison (1991) define *active learning* as "instructional activities involving students in doing things and thinking about what they are doing" (p. 5). Mills (2012) adds that for these two key components of active learning "students must engage in activities that involve reading, writing, discussing, or problem solving" (p. 1). In many of the activities suggested throughout this book, students can be engaged in several ways. In this chapter, activities include both in-class and out-of-class writing assignments.

In-Class Response Writing Tasks

Faculty at the LEARN Center (2017) at the University of Wisconsin-Whitewater suggest that one efficient way we can improve student writing is to "regularly assign brief writing exercises in [our] classes." Short writing exercises not only give students a chance to practice, they also help "students to become more active and self-aware learners" (Cadwell & Sorcinelli, 1997, p. 142).

The writing activities (or tasks) can be written for different learning levels as delineated in Bloom's Taxonomy of cognitive domains (see Figure 5.1). We can ask students to express their thoughts and ideas on a topic, answer different types of questions about content knowledge, make a free-write or journal entry, compare and contrast different views/content, apply content to different situations, or problem-solve.

So we will not be overwhelmed with many of our students' poor writing skills, we can just remind students to do their best because we will not be scoring their spelling, punctuation, or mechanics of writing. However, with free-writes, we can use these activities to give our students feedback on how they clarify ideas, identify key points, or explore concepts and issues. In doing so, we can help "students synthesize diverse ideas and identify points they may not understand" (LEARN Center, 2017). Free-writes can also guide us to make decisions on topics that might need to be addressed or readdressed at the next class.

An example of one activity that I use for in-class written responses and/or as a prewriting exercise for a short response paper is from Brookfield and Preskill (2005). They describe this activity as a way to encourage discussion and written responses from students, but I have also found it useful in helping students clarify concepts, brainstorm, cluster, and/or draft ideas for a short response paper. To set up the classroom for this activity, identify areas for the different "stations" and then put newsprint and felt tip or marking pens or a chalkboard and chalk at each station along with a prompt or question. At each station, groups

> are given 5 or 10 minutes to discuss a provocative issue and record their ideas on newsprint or a chalkboard. When this time is up the groups move to new positions in the classroom where they continue their discussion. But now the comments written on the newsprint or chalkboard by the preceding group at the station add a new voice to the mix. Rotations continue every 10 minutes until each group has been at all of the positions and has had a chance to consider all of the other groups' comments. (Brookfield & Preskill, 2005, p. 107)

Brookfield and Preskill (2005) suggest that we inform the student groups that it will be their responsibility (as a group) to put their answers and/or responses to the prompt or question on the newsprint or chalkboard. I let students make bullet points as long as their ideas are clearly understood, but I encourage them to use complete sentences. Once the time is up, I give a signal for the entire class so that each group can wrap up and get ready to move to the next station. As they move to the next station, the students are instructed to "continue [their] conversation by responding to the comments left behind by the group that has just vacated that station" (p. 107).

When using the rotating stations, I usually have every student participate in the writing (and also have the students put their initials under what they wrote); however, sometimes I ask the students in each group to take turns being the "recorder" at each station. The advantage of using rotating stations is that "the safety and intimacy of small groups is retained, yet the diversity of viewpoints experienced in a whole class discussion is incorporated . . . . Voices [are heard from and responded to] in a way that is less threatening than in large group exchanges" (Brookfield & Preskill, 2005,

p. 108). To conclude the rotating stations activity, at the end of the period, or at the start of the next class, I ask students to free write their own short responses to the material and/or concepts discussed at one or more of the rotating stations.

Another variation for handling the movement part of rotating stations is to set up 8 to 10 stations (numbering each) and use 2 prompts or questions—a prompt for even-numbered stations and another prompt for odd-numbered stations. When signaling the students to move, even-numbered groups move to an odd-numbered table and vice versa. This works well when time for the activity is limited. Each group receives 2 different prompts and has opportunities to respond to a different group's responses.

When using the rotating stations activity, we can increase the chances of students meeting and talking with others from different backgrounds by randomly assigning students to a small group. The benefit of doing this is that it breaks the typical habit of students just staying with students they are friends with or familiar with when they pick their own groups. In addition, the small-group work will not only facilitate students' interaction with their peers for the purpose of working on intellectual tasks, but it will also send a signal to the students that we value such interactions and recognize the benefits of them working together (Kuh et al., 2005).

For large classes (e.g., more than 60 students), the concept of Brookfield and Preskill's rotating stations can still be applied; however, with so many people, it can be difficult to have them physically move around a room. In this case, pocket folders can be used for sharing comments and responses from one small group with another. This is how it works: Questions (or prompts) are typed at the top of papers that are placed inside folders. Other directions can also be in each folder so that each group can read again what they are to do. As each group receives a folder, they discuss the topic, or the prompts, and write responses on the paper. A "round-robin style" of commenting can be used by passing around the paper in each small group so that each person can write a short response. Students will also talk about all the written comments. When the time is up, groups put their paper(s) with all their responses back in the folder, and all folders are passed to the next group so they can respond to what the previous group wrote and add new responses. The amount of time you want to devote to this activity will determine how many times the folders can be passed. For my classes, I try to have the folders passed to at least three groups, four if possible. In addition, all the folders are passed to the professor at the end of the exercise so comments can be reviewed.

Caldwell and Sorcinelli (1997) refer to the short writing tasks that students complete during class (such as those described previously) as "writing-to-learn" activities. They are also referred to as "low-stakes" activities because they are not graded in the way a traditional formal paper is graded. For some activities, such as rotating stations or passing of folders, it might be too cumbersome to have students turn in any "individual" responses, but we can move around the room to monitor and encourage participation. For other types of in-class writings, however, I have found using three-inch-by-five-inch cards very helpful. I have students write their individual answers or reflections on the cards. Not only are these cards easy to collect, but they stack up neatly and are easy to sort and read. By having students do this, the short writings can "help faculty gain insight into students' thinking and learning processes that will allow them to offer appropriate support and direction and provide more and better feedback to students without greater expenditure of time" (Caldwell & Sorcinelli, 1997, p. 148).

While low-stakes writings also give students a way to share with us "how they think and feel about different concepts and issues" (Centre for Teaching Excellence, n.d.a), Fink (2013) reminds us that all writing activities should be aligned with course learning objectives and goals. After students complete a short in-class writing, they can discuss and share their written responses with each other in small groups and/or in a whole-class discussion before they turn them in. Many professors use random calling so that two or three students do not dominate class discussions. "Professors who successfully integrate writing and critical thinking tasks into their courses often report [that] . . . class discussions are richer, students are more fully engaged in their learning and the quality of their performance improves" (Bean, 2001, p. 1).

Low-stakes writing assignments also help prepare students for answering the open-ended questions on exams. The Centre for Teaching Excellence (n.d.a) suggests that all short writings do not have to be read and graded by professors but that students can share writings with each other and give each other feedback. Short writings can help students as they "try to make [concepts] clear and accessible to others, in the process coming to understand the concepts better themselves" (Centre for Teaching Excellence, n.d.a).

When considering one's course goals and objectives, Rendon (2006) argues that "teaching and learning for the future must take into consideration the complex and diverse nature of students today" (p. 16). In doing so, Rendon recommends that professors bring in additional resources and speakers so that the class curriculum includes multicultural content, not just views from Western civilization. In classes with a safe and trusting climate, and where professors have fostered a community of learners, it is hoped that minority, first-generation, and academically unprepared students will have the opportunity to have their voices heard. Low-stakes writing-to-learn tasks are especially effective when helping our students expand their horizons and broaden their worldviews.

Out-of-Class Reflective Writing Tasks

In addition to in-class writings, assigning short papers to be completed outside of class (homework) is effective for promoting learning and improving writing skills. Fink (2013) calls these assignments reflective writings. The value of these kinds of writings (as well as the in-class short response writings) is that they help "the writer become more self-conscious about learning. Becoming more aware of themselves as learners starts the process of allowing students to become self-directing and meaning-making learners" (Fink, 2013, p. 130).

The out-of-class reflective topics can be related to content covered in class and/or related topics. For example, I have assigned short videos (e.g., educational TED Talks that relate to the course) and supplemental readings as homework, and students must then write a reflective response to the material. An excellent example of different prompts or questions that we can use comes from a history teacher. He asks his students the following questions about the assigned reading:

> When did the author write? To what audience? Under what personal/ professional circumstances?
> What was the author trying to accomplish by writing?
> On what topics do you trust the author? On what not at all? Where do you take the author with a grain of salt?
> Take any one of the guiding questions for the course from the first page of our course syllabus. How does this reading help answer it? (Caldwell & Sorcinelli, 1997, p. 145)

Short reflective or response papers can be assigned several times throughout the semester as homework. For me, I require students to submit a hard copy in class, but before turning it in, the students can refer to it during a small-group discussion (as mentioned in chapter 6). Some professors have their students submit their work online.

In lower division classes with more than 30 students, I have generally limited the students' reflective papers to one page for three reasons. First, the assignment is a low-stakes assignment in that it is worth a small percentage of points for the final grade, so students who struggle with writing are not overwhelmed or stressed as opposed to writing a high-stakes paper worth a large percentage of the final grade points. Second, I can comment and correct these papers fairly quickly for grammar, spelling, punctuation, sentence structure, American Psychological Association (APA) guidelines, and so on, allowing me to give the papers back to the students the very next week. Third, once papers are returned, I offer the students a chance to make corrections and resubmit the paper for more points if they did not earn an A or B on the assignment. Thus, by making revisions and corrections, students can improve their writing skills before they write their next paper or start on a major high-stakes term paper (discussed next).

Considering the fact that many students start the semester with poor writing skills and have limited "prior experience with writing and the complex nature of writing . . . [professors can use the short reflection papers to] provide support as students continue to hone their skills" (Eberly Center, 2008). To help students move forward, I use the following procedure for revising papers and resubmitting them:

1. The student receives corrective feedback on his or her typed reflection paper; corrective feedback means that the mechanical errors (e.g., punctuation, spelling, capitalization, sentence fragments, or run-ons) are circled and any other notes from the professor (or teaching assistant) are written in the margins.
2. The student makes corrections on his or her paper and highlights on the first version each part that is being revised or corrected and prints out the new corrected paper.
3. The student turns in both the new and the original paper (stapled together) within one week of when the paper was returned to him or her. The revised paper will not be accepted or read unless the original paper is attached and errors are highlighted on the old paper.

When rescoring reflective papers, I can easily look for the changes students have made by comparing the two versions, and it is a fairly fast process. To help students improve in their writing skills, I believe it is imperative to allow revisions for poorly written papers. By letting students make revisions, we can "meet students where they are in terms of their academic preparation, developmental level and motivation" (Laird et al., 2008, p. 96) and give them an opportunity to succeed.

In addition, these assignments have a "direct correlation between effort and outcome" (Morales, 2014, p. 96), and they allow early success with effort, which corresponds to strengthening students' confidence and self-efficacy. Morales (2014) found that for students of color from low socioeconomic backgrounds, the greatest strength for overcoming the high odds of failure was academic resilience, which is supported by having a strong sense of self-efficacy. As professors, we can impact the retention of low socioeconomic students by giving "heavily *effort based* assignments" early in the semester (Morales, 2014, p. 96).

To ensure that all students, even those with good writing skills, do not misuse the revision policy, I also have a policy that the points awarded on revisions can improve their grade only by one and a half letter grades. For example, a D paper can be resubmitted for a C+, but not higher. This policy helps students turn in their best effort the first time.

Both out-of-class reflective writings and in-class writings are activities where students are "writing to learn," but they are also tasks where students are "learning to write" by correcting and revising papers that are scored below a satisfactory grade. Without doing this, many will continue to make the same mistakes. Thus, by assigning several reflective papers, students will be able to improve their writing skills before they start working on a high-stakes term or research paper, which in many college courses are not due until the last few weeks of the semester. In addition, Reason and colleagues (2006) suggest that faculty can "promote active student engagement with their courses' content, requiring students to participate actively in classes and to write multiple iterations of papers, and to come into contact with diverse peoples, cultures, and ideas" (p. 170). Thus, when students bring in their writings, we can put them in diverse small groups to share their response papers.

We can also give students assistance during office hours or other arranged times. During our office hours, we can schedule students and work with them individually or in small groups. I have found that these meetings have "been particularly constructive for [academically] unprepared students. Most at-risk students respond in a positive way" (Gabriel, 2008, p. 31). In addition, students can seek help through the university's writing or tutoring services.

Substantive Formal Writing: Procrastination and Plagiarism

Fink (2013) defines *substantive writing assignments* as "writing that is focused on a topic and that attempts to present an organized statement about the information and ideas the writer has about that topic" (p. 129). Furthermore, an intensive writing project can "encourage students to invest significant and meaningful time and effort on authentic, complex tasks over an extended period of time" (Centre for Teaching Excellence, n.d.b). By going through the experience of writing a major paper, a component of higher education's high-impact practices, students have the opportunity to enhance their writing skills as well as their quantitative reasoning skills (Sandeen, 2012, p. 87).

When including a research component as part of the intensive writing project, term papers (also referred to as research or capstone papers) in the traditional form involve students using research skills in order to find appropriate sources, and then selecting quotes from the sources as evidence, which will be incorporated into their papers. One problem often associated with term papers is procrastination. As Weimer (2002) points out we have "students who procrastinate and attempt to complete term-long projects in one night" (p. 96). So, what can we do to minimize this problem?

To begin, Huba and Freed (2000) suggest that we need to give clear, explicit directions and a rubric that "explains to students the criteria against which their work will be judged . . . [and which] makes public key criteria that students can use in developing, revising, and judging their own work" (p. 155). A detailed rubric that explains the criteria for each component of the term or research paper is especially valuable for historically underrepresented students who are also first generation and academically unprepared, because many of these students have very little, if any, experience writing a research paper.

The directions along with the rubric will provide guidance throughout the writing process. As Gehr (2005) notes,

> Use grading criteria or rubrics to set a tone of encouragement rather than punishment. Define the terms that you use in these rubrics. If you ask for a "reasonably complex" thesis statement, provide an example of what one looks like . . . . Ask questions rather than giving commands, emphasize what an effective paper does rather than what a lousy paper does not do, and arrange criteria from most to least important. (p. 1)

However, giving students explicit directions and a rubric that spells out the different components and criteria still might not prevent them from procrastinating. We can also advise students that writing a term or research paper is a process and hard work (LEARN Center, 2017), but despite our advice and warnings ("Do not wait until the last minute to write this paper!"), many students do not start working on their papers until the due date is very near.

Light (2001) suggests that we need to recognize that one of the biggest problems college students have is poor time management, and often this becomes one of the major reasons why they struggle in college. Students who manage their time poorly improperly prioritize what needs to be done, do not set aside adequate time to complete assignments, and put off what they need to do. Procrastination has a negative impact on learning and grades. Ackerman and Gross (2005) note the following: "Although procrastination is not always detrimental to performance (Lay, 1986) and is moderated by other variables such as cognitive ability (Beck, Koons, & Milgrim, 2000), numerous studies have found procrastination related to lower grade point average, lower performance on specific assignments, and lower achievement in individual classes" (p. 6). Thus, procrastination can lead to poor performance in classes, which can also lead to disengagement, which can lead to eventual dropping out or academic dismissal.

As professors, we can help our students avoid procrastination when it comes to completing a major term or research paper. Ackerman and Gross (2005) note that professors can "help students not to procrastinate by breaking up large semester-long assignments into smaller interdependent ones" (p. 10). The smaller interdependent parts, or *installments*, as Ackerman and Gross call them, can have earlier due dates. Once students turn in the first installment, we can also give students feedback. Then, they can make corrections before the next part is due. As students turn in installments and receive feedback, they can make improvements on each part before putting all the parts together to turn in the final large assignment. For example, I have broken up a term paper for a lower division class into six parts (not including the title and reference page) as follows:

1. Introduction for entire paper
2. Part 1A—Description/characteristics of first condition (with at least two references)
3. Part 1B—Application and one solution to first condition (using same references from 1A)
4. Part 2A—Description/characteristics of second condition (with at least two additional references—not those used in parts 1A and 1B)
5. Part 2B—Application and one solution of second condition (using same references from 2A)
6. Conclusion for entire paper

First, students have to turn in their topic and the titles of at least two references for the first part of the paper. Next, about a week later, students have to turn in a completed part of the paper (e.g., part 1A or part 1B). This happens about five weeks before the total paper is due. I read, give corrective feedback (especially on citations and proper use of APA format), and return this first installment to the students. The length of each part is limited to two typed double-spaced pages. Then, about a week after the first installment has been returned, students turn in a second "installment" of the paper. Again, I read and give corrective feedback and return. The students now have two parts of the paper done. About two weeks later, the entire paper is due, and the first parts with my corrective comments must be turned in with the final paper. This procedure also benefits me—the time it takes to grade the final paper is much less than it used to be because two parts have already been corrected. With students turning in the first and second installments with the final paper, I can quickly check to make sure that proper corrections were made. Another benefit is that students learn to improve their writing when they have to make corrections on what was turned in, so the last components of their papers have fewer errors and overall show a higher quality of writing.

In addition, I find this procedure especially beneficial for academically at-risk students and/or anyone who has trouble with time management. By breaking up the large assignment into smaller steps, or installments, that have to be turned in, we can quickly find out who is behind or has not started on the assignment. Reaching out to students who have not turned in the first installment is a way we can intervene and help them get on track. We can ask those students to meet with us after class, or we can follow up with an e-mail asking them for a meeting during office hours (or another time that works). I am not suggesting that professors accept or grade late assignments if they do not want to. What I am suggesting is that talking to students who do not turn in the smaller portion of the larger assignment is a way to troubleshoot why those students have not done so. It is also a good time to have students "recommit" to the class.

Another benefit of having students turn in installments is that "students are less likely to suddenly come up with a product that is plagiarized or fabricated" (Gabriel, 2008, p. 107). Unfortunately, there are many ways for students to order a free paper or buy a term paper from online or even local resources.[1] Harris (2015) points out that "some students are just procrastinators, while others do not understand the hours required to develop a good research paper, and they run out of time as the due date looms. Thus, they are most tempted to copy a paper when time is short, and they have not yet started the assignment" (p. 1).

To address the time factor that students often are not aware of, Ambrose and colleagues (2010) suggest giving students a checklist. Checklists are helpful "because students do not always fully understand our expectations, and they may be guided by disciplinary or cultural conventions, or even the expectations of other instructors, that mismatch with what we expect for the current activity or assignment" (p. 255). Even though we give our students explicit instructions and a rubric, they can benefit from a checklist that they fill out, sign, and turn in with the final paper (or project). Ambrose and colleagues note that such a checklist will also assist them in recognizing how much time completing a major term or research paper will take. Checklists might include several components that you expect the students to address in their paper as well as format and other requirements (Ambrose et al., 2010). Examples of items that might be used on a checklist include the following: I have covered each subtopic; I have used four sources and listed all of them in the reference page; I have included examples and quotes to support my thesis; I have checked my subtopic headings (following the format requirements for APA style); I have completed a "spelling and grammar" check and have carefully read my final version of this paper. Once students go through the checklist and put a "check" by each statement, we can ask them to sign and attach the completed checklist to their paper.

Another action that we, the professors, can take to help our students with major substantive writing assignments is to use the college's or university's writing center or labs. Morales (2014) reported the following:

> Instead of waiting for students to struggle and suggesting or hoping they make an appointment, some faculty required students to take at least one paper to the writing lab before submitting it. Not only did this help improve student writing, but it also made certain students know where and how tutoring appointments took place. Many students only went to tutoring initially because they had to, but then made it part of their weekly or monthly routine. Faculty members who do not want to require it, could make a visit to the writing center worth extra points. Either way, getting students there initially often made a significant difference. (p. 99)

Morales notes that making sure students get support at a writing center can be crucial for low socioeconomic students because many of these "students in particular are often less likely to be engaged in outside class activities, such as study groups, and informal interactions with faculty" (p. 99). When we encourage our students to develop "help-seeking tendencies," we are helping our students develop a resilience attitude.

Morales (2014) further explains that resilience factors can be crucial as minority and low-income students seek to overcome the high odds of not making it to graduation. Resilience is closely related to a growth mindset and mental toughness (see chapter 4 for further discussion). "Essentially, educational resilience is the statistically anomalous academic achievement of students who possess and confront 'risk factors' that predict failure for most students from similar circumstances" (Morales, 2014, p. 93). Being able to complete a major writing project that is a significant portion of one's grade is a part of many college courses, and students need to know that they can learn how to become efficient and capable writers through effort and by seeking help in order to receive corrective feedback.

Discouraging Plagiarism and Encouraging Scrutiny of Sources

For short or long papers, plagiarism and having appropriate sources are two major concerns that many professors have when they assign a paper. To begin, many of us have a statement regarding "academic integrity" on our syllabi, which also includes the college or university policy for violations. This is considered a standard procedure at many institutions. In addition, we can discuss plagiarism in class with our students. As recommended by Gabriel (2008),

> First, take some class time to discuss plagiarism. Go over plagiarism definitions, why it is important, and how to avoid plagiarism. Some students will plagiarize by accident, carelessness, or just not understanding the "rules" of proper citation or acceptable paraphrasing. By going over these things in class, we can let students know that such excuses are not acceptable. (p. 108)

Online plagiarism tutorials, such as *You Be the Judge* and *Plagiarism: It's Your Call*, are also available, and students can complete these as homework.[2] I have found both of these interactive programs to be very successful in raising students' awareness of plagiarism and their knowledge on how to properly document their sources. There are many other resources available to help us raise our students' knowledge of and awareness of plagiarism. For example, we can share with our students a short article (with a long title) "Nine Things You Should Already Know About PLAGIARISM Plus . . . Six Excuses That Don't Work and . . . Three Things You Don't Need to Worry About" from the Integrity Center at the University of Oklahoma (n.d.). The information in this article can help our students understand why plagiarism is something they must avoid.

For faculty, an informative resource called "Plagiarism Detection and Prevention: An Instructor Guide" is available from Penn State's Teaching and Learning With Technology (n.d.a) web page. One of the specific topics in the instructor's guide is called "Why Students Plagiarize" (Penn State, n.d.b). Considering the "why" can be helpful for us as we assign papers and take steps to prevent plagiarism. Among the reasons listed that some students plagiarize is students' lack of planning and/or not understanding the citation rules. However, other reasons include a lack of interest in the assignments and a perception that cheating is easy because professors will not check or enforce the rules. Ways to counter students' lack of planning and a lack of understanding citation rules have already been addressed. We can also take steps to counter students' lack of interest in the assignment and their perceptions that cheating is easy.

First, to counter some students' lack of interest, Ackerman and Gross (2005) advise us to "be cognizant of student career interests and develop assignments that provide students with opportunities to develop career-relevant knowledge and skills" (p. 10). They also note that students will start earlier on assignments that they find interesting and when there is a choice within the acceptable limits. By starting early and being interested in their topic, students are less likely to order, buy, or fabricate a paper. When they are personally interested and vested in the topic, students are also less likely to plagiarize.

Second, to counter the notion that professors will not check for plagiarism, I recommend using Turnitin.com or other resources that will detect plagiarism and letting students know that all papers must first be submitted to this type of plagiarism-checking program. The Turnitin technology is available to many colleges and universities, and I have it set up on my courses' Blackboard Learn page. All students are required to use it before each installment due date, and then they can "correct" any plagiarism mistakes. Once they make corrections, the students resubmit their paper. The objective here is to make sure they have the feedback to make corrections before the final due date. In addition, the "originality" and "similar percentage" features of the program are valuable tools because they alert students (and the professor) when they have used too many quotes and need to do more of their own writing in their paper.

Using appropriate sources is another concern. When assigning writing projects, college and university professors often ask students to use scholarly or peer-reviewed sources. For lower division classes, many professors will use class time to explain the difference between a scholarly source and a popular periodical. However, whether the course is a lower or upper division course, consider assigning students a short video to watch as homework. There are several excellent videos to choose from (available on YouTube) that are authored by librarians from different universities. A sample of videos available for professors to choose from is as follows:

Carnegie Vincent Library. (2013). *Scholarly and Popular Sources*. Retrieved from https://www.youtube.com/watch?v=tN8S4CbzGXU

Vanderbilt University. (2017). *Scholarly vs. Popular Periodicals*. Retrieved from https://www.youtube.com/watch?v=ysPDZGj3cRA

North Central Texas College Libraries. (2013). *Scholarly Journals vs. Popular Magazines*. Retrieved from https://www.youtube.com/watch?v=2TohbuWsctE

The videos have examples of scholarly and peer-reviewed journals and explain how these articles are different from articles in popular periodicals or magazines. The videos also give students tips on what to look for so they can distinguish between these two types of published articles.

It is also important to discuss with our students other sources beyond academic journals and popular periodicals. In helping to prepare our students for an overwhelming bombardment of mass media and Internet sources, including Twitter, Facebook, and Snapchat, I believe we must expand our discussion to help them examine and evaluate these types of material that they are constantly exposed to and use in their everyday lives. Many of our students expect to be able to gather content immediately and even endlessly and often do not look at where the content comes from, the reliability of the source, or whether it has been fabricated (as noted in the previous chapter). Teaching students how to detect false or misleading information is something that we must address. Purdue Online Writing Lab (2013) advises readers, "Evaluating sources of information is an important step in any research activity." Thus, it provides information on how readers can evaluate different types of sources including Internet sources, bibliographic citations, and print versus Internet sources.

It may also be worthwhile to devote some class time to having a discussion about "fake news," even though most research or term papers do not allow popular periodicals, newspapers, or online web pages as sources. Given the increased exposure of mass media, misinformation, fake news, and so on, I believe it can be beneficial for our students to evaluate different types of media outlets and apply critical thinking skills about such sources. For example, Cable News Network (CNN) recently published articles and videos on how to fact-check and how to spot fake news. Holan (2016) points out that "fake news, the phenomenon that is now sweeping, well, the news . . . is made-up stuff, masterfully manipulated to look like credible journalistic reports that are easily spread online to large audiences willing to believe the fictions and spread the word" (p. 1) and also suggests examining such sites as PolitiFact.com. Finally, Kiely and Robertson (2016), authors for FactCheck.org, provide the following guidelines for spotting unreliable articles:

- Consider the source.
- Read beyond the headline.
- Check the author.
- What's the support?

- Check the date.
- Is this some kind of joke (or satire)?
- Check your biases.
- Consult the experts. (FactCheck.org)

When citing research and sources, students must be vigilant in ensuring that they are credible. If we promote vetting of sources and research in our everyday lives and encourage students to think critically about the information they are consuming (and where it is coming from), this critical thinking will invariably carry over into more traditional research and sourcing used in term papers in our courses.

Conclusion

Writing is an important part of one's higher education, and regardless of whether students begin college with adequate writing skills, as professors we can do several things to assist our students in becoming proficient writers. Brockman, Taylor, Kreth, and Crawford (2011) found that most faculty "generally agreed that the purpose behind most writing assignments is to help students learn class concepts and, further, that assignments either foster or require an ability to read, understand, and manage source materials" (p. 77). Bean (2001) reminds us that "emphasizing writing and critical thinking in a course increases the amount of subject matter that students actually learn and in many cases can actually *increase total coverage* of content" (p. 9; emphasis in original). By using both low-stakes writing-to-learn tasks in class and reflective writings outside of class with corrective feedback and revisions, we can help *all* students be engaged in class, increase their learning, and at the same time develop their writing. Writing-to-learn assignments can promote critical thinking, independent learning, focused thoughts, reflections, and retention of new information and ideas. In addition, these tasks can help students prepare for high-stakes writing assignments such as term or research papers, where the writing is formal, structured, and integrates course material with other sources.

As outlined in this chapter, we can do several things to help our minority, first-generation, low-income, and academically unprepared students. We can design our assignments in a way that holds students to high standards, but, at the same time, we can give all our students encouragement, support, and resources so that they have ample opportunity to achieve those standards.

Notes

1. For example, there are websites such as www.boostmygrade.com advertising that they can not only write papers, but also take exams for online students; another example is www.takeyourclass.com, whose services go beyond just writing a paper for a price.

2. *You Be the Judge* can be found at www.fairfield.edu/library/services/instruction/plagiarismtutorial/. *Plagiarism: It's Your Call* can be found at http://skil.stanford.edu/module6/paraphrasing.html.

8

RESILIENCE, HABITS, AND PERSISTENCE

Hold Fast and See It Through

A total commitment is paramount to reaching the ultimate in performance.

—*Tom Flores (1937–)*

Introduction

As noted in the first chapter of this book, colleges and universities have a graduation gap: "The odds of succeeding in college are stacked against certain types of students. Disproportionate numbers of those who drop out are from historically underserved groups" (Laird et al., 2008, p. 85). Seeking ways to close the gap between traditionally served students and historically underserved groups such as minority students, first-generation students, academically unprepared students, and even low-income students has become a top priority for many. Pascarella and Terenzini (2005) suggest that "the impact of college is largely determined by individual efforts and involvement in the academic, interpersonal, and extracurricular offerings on a campus . . . [and] students . . . bear major responsibility for any gain they derive from their post secondary experience" (p. 602). However, what is missing from this statement is that the playing field is not level, and, hence, the amount of effort that is needed (along with tenacity and perseverance) is much greater for some than others.

As professors, I believe we can make a difference when it comes to helping our most vulnerable students put forth the necessary effort to be involved in our classes and have a positive learning experience. Can we impact everyone who enrolls in our classes or with whom we have contact? Of course not. Still, we have a great responsibility and vital role when it comes to improving retention, persistence, and success rates at each of our institutions. As we set up our classes, the decisions we make about which teaching methods we will use, how we will interact with our students, and even how we will reach out to them, can inspire many of our students to put forth their best effort. We can be encouraging and supportive and give them guidance on how they can help themselves, especially those students who have traditionally had very low success rates.

Unfortunately, Fleming (2012) found that "the educational landscape is still marred by hostile educational environments, stereotypical expectations, and a failure to nurture" (p. 3). Each of us must examine our own shortcomings and biases. We must guard against having such negative factors in our classrooms. In doing so, we not only become better teachers but also have a positive impact on the culture of our campuses. Retention efforts work when we have positive "interactions among students, faculty and staff . . . . Retention is manufactured in classrooms by satisfied students, in interactions with caring faculty . . . [and] retention thus becomes a by-product of learning" (p. 76). From increased retention, we have a chance to close the graduation gap.

This is an awesome task. I am not trying to be a Pollyanna purist; I do not believe everyone who comes to our doorstep will pass our classes, persist in college, and graduate. However, we should be careful to avoid prejudging who can or cannot succeed in college. Weimer (2011) believes one of the worst mistakes a teacher can make is to decide who can learn and who cannot. She tells us that as professors we should not prejudge who can pass our course or succeed in a certain major (or field) and who cannot, even when we observe a student demonstrating behaviors that are compromising his or her success in a course (e.g., missing class, not doing homework, failing the first exam).

Even for students who are not doing what they should be doing to be successful, that does not mean they cannot turn it around and learn the material. Weimer (2011) advises that "the consequences of this mistake [assuming who can and can not learn] are very significant for students. Avoid this mistake by recognizing that you do the teaching and students do the learning" (p. 12). At the same time, we need to be honest with our students about where they are currently and where they need to be and even articulate steps that they need to take to master the course material. Weimer notes, "We have a responsibility to guide and inform students" (p. 5).

Throughout this book, I have presented several ways that we can guide and inform our students. In this chapter, I focus on three additional precise factors that can positively influence the performance of all students, but especially minority, first-generation, and academically unprepared students: (a) building academic resilience, (b) developing positive habits and routines, and (c) promoting Productive Persistence.

Building Academic Resilience

Yeager and Dweck (2012) define *resilience* as "students respond[ing] positively to challenges" and believe it is "crucial for success in school and in life" (p. 302). In his study, Morales (2014) found that promoting academic resilience can "increase the retention and graduation of . . . [our] most statistically at-risk students" (p. 92) in higher education. Morales determined four broad categories that professors could specifically act on to encourage academic resilience. Two of these categories have already been discussed in previous chapters: constantly build students' self-efficacy and encourage help-seeking tendencies. Two additional ways to build students' academic resilience are helping students realistically appraise their own strengths and weaknesses and providing clear links between academic success and future economic security (Morales, 2014).

Self-Appraisal of Academic Strengths and Weaknesses

When considering ways we can help students appraise their own strengths and weaknesses in a realistic manner, we have to be careful. As professors, we want to support students and give them praise, but we also do not want to mislead students by failing to tell them where they need to improve. For example, I had a student who told me she wanted to be a doctor, but she had also received approval for a "course substitution" for college algebra from the office of Disabled Student Services. College algebra, however, was a prerequisite for many of the science classes that need to be taken in preparation for the medical school entrance exam (MCAT), and because of the course substitution she could not register for these classes. When she came to my office, I had to be frank and honest with her that if she could not get over her fear of math and pass the college algebra class, she would not be able to take the necessary science classes to prepare for the MCAT. I never told her she could not do it; I just helped her understand what she had to do. At the same time, we discussed other "helping" professions that she might be interested in pursuing. It turned out that after a semester of math with math tutoring she decided on another professional goal. Upon graduation from college, she became a counselor at a shelter for battered women and children. The point is that she had to assess her own weakness and decided how to respond.

Using formative assessments and discussing the results with students can also help them realize their strengths and weaknesses and what they still need to do before the *real* exam (Gabriel, 2008). Ungraded formative assessments are also valuable for us, the professors, because we may be able to find out before the exam key concepts that the majority of the class has not grasped. By knowing this ahead of time, we can adjust our teaching schedule or the review session that we have planned. After the exam is given and students receive their results, meeting with students individually who received a D or lower can be an effective way to get students back on the right track for passing the next exam (McBrayer, 2001). During such meetings, reviewing course material is helpful, but discussing ways the student prepares for the exam and his or her other study habits can be even more beneficial.

Another excellent post exam activity that promotes self-reflection and metacognition is the exam wrapper. Lovett (2013), in conjunction with some Carnegie Mellon professors, created exam wrappers, which are "structured reflection activities that prompt students to practice key metacognitive skills after they get back their grades" (p. 18). Many times we have seen students focusing only on their score, or grade, and not taking the time to contemplate how their own study strategies helped or hurt their performance on the exam.

When we give students the activity of completing an exam wrapper, we ask them to answer questions about the following areas: "(a) how they prepared for the exam, (b) what kinds of errors they made on the exam, and (c) what they might do differently to prepare for the next exam" (Lovett, 2013, p. 18). When students think about their own learning and their own learning strategies, they are participating in a metacognitive activity—thinking about their own learning. By having students participate in this metacognitive exercise, we are using the exam as not only an evaluation or an assessment for a grade but also a way to promote learning. Lovett (2013) provides several examples of exam wrappers that most of us can easily adapt to our own course, and they do not take up much class time (less than four minutes).

From the examples that Lovett (2013) provides, I created the exam wrapper in Figure 8.1 for a lower division educational course that I teach. The exam was an open-book and notes test.

College grades are a large part of the higher education experience. "Despite the limitations and problems in using them, Pascarella and Terenzini (2005) concluded that college grades are probably the best predictor of student persistence, degree completion, and graduate school enrollment" (Kuh et al., 2006, p. 76). When we give students assignments and exams, we are determining the ways we will evaluate and grade our students. In learning-centered teaching, Weimer (2002) notes that "evaluation is used to generate grades and to promote learning" (p. 119), and with the emphasis on learning, the purpose of grades becomes better balanced. Still, "grades matter very much in the short term, and only naïve faculty make proclamations to the contrary. But learning still matters more, especially in the long run" (Weimer, 2002, p. 120). By using exam wrappers, we can promote "self-regulated"

Figure 8.1. Sample exam wrapper.

---

1) Approximately how much time did you spend preparing for this exam? _____

2) What did you do to prepare for the test? Percentage of time . . .

• Reading textbook for first time _____

• Rereading section(s) _____

• Review class notes/handouts_____

• Reviewing material from course website _____

• Other _____

3) Now that you looked at your score . . . estimate the % you lost due to (must add up to 100)

• Trouble with understanding the concept? _____

• Not knowing where to find information in the text/notes? _____

• Not much experience with multiple choice or short answer exams_____

• Didn't spend enough time prereading or rereading sections _____

• Didn't spend enough time on checking my answers in the text _____

• Didn't read the whole question and/or all the answers carefully _____

4) Name three things you plan to do differently in preparing for the next exam.

5) What can I do to help support your learning and preparation for the next exam?

Note. Adapted from Lovett's Exam Wrapper Sample, 2013, pp. 42–43.

learning and put the emphasis not only on learning but also on self-evaluation of how one is learning.

In particular, students who have historically been underserved and underrepresented seem to benefit a great deal from exam wrappers. Many of these students are high risk "because they are expected to show greater independence and self-management in their learning, at the same time they are encountering new difficulties associated with college life and college-level material" (Lovett, 2013, p. 19). After completing the exam wrapper, students turn in their responses. Ambrose and colleagues (2010) note that "when students learn to reflect on the effectiveness of their own approach, they are able to identify problems and make the necessary adjustments" (p. 210).

I have students complete the exam wrapper as soon as their exams are returned. Then, once I read their exam wrapper answers, I return them to the students so they can refer to them as they prepare for the next exam. Ambrose and colleagues (2010) note that students will then have a "reminder of what they learned from their prior exam experience that can help them study more effectively" (p. 211). Not only are exam wrappers an effective way to help students appraise their strengths and weaknesses for preparing for exams, but they can also be used for other assignments or projects. Overall, the exam wrapper activity can contribute to students' academic resilience.

Academic Success and Future Economic Security Connections

Another way to build students' academic resilience is providing clear linkages between academic success and future economic security (Morales, 2014). Whether the information comes from the career center or from professors, Morales found that "the connection between academic performance and economic security proved to be an essential ingredient for resilience" (p. 100). We can bring real-world vocational topics and issues into our courses, including "speakers from career fields related to [our] . . . academic disciplines, creating assignments where students [have] to explore concepts inherent to prospective careers . . . and pointing out the value of early and constant resume building" (Morales, 2014, p. 100). When students recognize the connection between college and a career, especially one that will secure their economic future, motivated in class, they are not only more motivated in class but also usually exert more effort. All of this can result in our students increasing their academic resilience, which can help them complete the courses that are especially challenging and difficult to do well in, yet are required for graduation.

Developing Positive Habits and Routines

As noted in chapter 3, developing positive habits, such as attending class regularly, can help students with their grades and positively impact college retention. Because the majority of today's students live off campus and commute to school, "the classroom is the only venue where they regularly have face-to-face contact with faculty or staff members and other students" (Laird et al., 2008, p. 86).

For most lower division courses, classes are scheduled to meet on specific days and times every week of the semester, and most meet at least 2 or 3 times a week for at least 50 minutes. Even classes that meet only once a week will have a 3-hour meeting for a 3-unit class. This contact assumes that classes are not canceled and that students attend. Of course, during the semester, someone is bound to miss a class for a legitimate reason. As professors we can help develop undergraduate students' positive habit of attending class, as well as bringing their textbook(s) and other supplies.

"Routines can be incredibly complex or fantastically simple" (Duhigg, 2012, p. 25). Routines come from repeated patterns, so requiring students to bring the textbook once in a while will probably mean that a lot of students will forget to bring their book to class. However, when we ask students to always bring their text, and then use it at some point during every class, then the vast majority of students will incorporate that behavior as part of their attendance habit.

Duhigg (2012) explains how habits are shaped from repeated patterns that we develop and continually implement. According to Duhigg, habits have the following three-step loop:

> First there is a *cue*, a trigger that tells your brain to go into automatic mode and which habit to use. Then there is *routine*, which can be physical or mental or emotional. Finally there is a *reward*, which helps your brain figure out if this particular loop is worth remembering for the future . . . . Over time, this loop—cue, routine, reward . . . becomes more and more automatic. (p. 19)

So what does a habit have to do with class attendance? If students repeat the pattern of attending class every day and bringing their textbook(s) and supplies, then going to class can become a habit. As professors, we can help create attendance patterns by always holding class, always starting class on time, and always ending class on time.

Duhigg (2012) notes, "When a habit emerges, the brain stops fully participating in decision-making. It stops working so hard, or diverts focus to other tasks" (p. 20). Thus, students who are in the habit of going to class will be less likely to be distracted by other activities on campus that might keep them from going to class, or from forgetting to go to class. (Yes, this can happen, especially for classes that meet only once a week.) Students' time-use habits can influence their academic performance. When students increased their "time and engagement with structured learning activities," their grades and course completion improved (Fleming, 2012, p. 5).

If classes are randomly canceled (even for an alternative assignment such as an online module) only once a semester it is not a problem, but if it happens several times a semester, it can affect students' overall attendance by interrupting their "habit" or routine of coming to class. Of course, there may be a time when a professor experiences an unexpected illness or a family emergency and finds that canceling a class is unavoidable. In this rare instance, we should try to contact students ahead of time. Always being "present" for class meetings is a way for us to model for our students the same behavior that we want from them. If a professor cancels several classes in a semester, it can send a message that class is not that important. It can also disrupt a student's routine, and, consequently, he or she can accidentally miss a class meeting. Braxton (2006) points out that "college attendance shapes social skills and personal habits important for adult living. The development of such skills and habits supplies us with a set of indicators of college student success" (p. 5).

In addition to having a cue and a routine, the third component in creating a habit is to clearly define the reward. As professors, we can assist our students in recognizing or even clarifying the many possible rewards that they can receive from being in class. Rewards can range from tangible or concrete items (e.g., food, extra information or bonus material given out, points or credit that counts toward the final grade) to "emotional payoffs, such as the feelings of pride that accompany praise or self-congratulation" (Duhigg, 2012, p. 25). Instead of warning our students of the consequences of missing class, we need to stress the message of the rewards for attending class. Students who attend classes often get a handout or extra information that is not posted on the class web page until later. Always having an engaging educational activity to elaborate, clarify, or apply the course content is another type of reward that students receive for being present in class. "By being engaged, students develop habits that promise to stand them in good stead for a lifetime of continuous learning" (Laird et al., 2008, p. 87).

Reason and colleagues (2006) found that "students' interactions with faculty members" had the greatest impact for promoting student success and persistence (p. 151). Class meetings are a way that we can ensure we have a consistent and reliable way of interacting with our students. When students know that class will always be held, not canceled or substituted with an online assignment, then they will also put more value on their own class attendance. When examining various factors that affect students' retention, Reason and colleagues (2006) also noted that students who felt "faculty and staff at their institution provided the academic and non-academic support they needed, and who felt they had good relationships with faculty members and administrative staff, were more likely than similar students at other institutions to report greater gains in academic competence" (p. 16).

For struggling and unprepared students, the habit of going to class has a potentially even greater value. It is from our contact with students in class that we can set up appointments or conferences to also meet with them *out-side* of class. As Chickering and Gamson (1987) point out,

Frequent student-faculty contact in and out of classes is the most important factor in student motivation and involvement. Faculty concern helps students get through rough times and keep on working. Knowing a few faculty members well enhances students' intellectual commitment and encourages them to think about their own values and future plans. (p. 3)

Finally, all habits have another necessary ingredient that is critical. That ingredient is belief (Duhigg, 2012). Students have to believe that attending class really does help them and is therefore worth their time and effort to be there. Thus, what happens in class must connect not only to our learning outcomes or objectives but also the course assessments. Whether we use tests, exams, research papers, reflection papers, projects, or other assessments, they should connect to what is covered in class even if they also include other assignments (e.g., readings and writings) that students are required to complete outside of class. The attendance habit can be valuable for our students and for us as we seek to get our students engaged in our classes.

Promoting Productive Persistence

Productive Persistence is a term coined by the Carnegie Foundation for the Advancement of Teaching in their work with students in developmental mathematics courses. Beattie (2015), director of the project, noted that the framework for the program developed was "the result of an ongoing partnership where faculty regularly team up with leading psychology professors to combine academic research with practitioners' expertise."

Even though their research was with students in developmental math courses, their findings can be applied to many other academic fields. The term *Productive Persistence* "focuses on addressing student beliefs about themselves as . . . learners and doers, and their feeling of belonging in a . . . [learning] environment" (Beattie, 2015). The framework was to develop an action plan in response to students who typically give up as soon as the semester begins. They wanted to be able to help these students continue to work on their academics, both in time and in effort, even when they were struggling and facing challenges. They also wanted the students to use effective learning strategies when they did put forth effort. The Productive Persistence framework included the students attending class consistently; completing assignments, or time-on-task; engaging in help-seeking behaviors; learning from their errors; continuing to show effort even after failure; revising their work; and embracing the challenge of mastering the material.

To help students develop Productive Persistence behaviors, they first addressed beliefs about learning (see Figure 8.2 for all the components of

Figure 8.2. Productive Persistence framework.

Aim: Students continue to put forth effort during challenges and when they do so they use effective strategies.	Students believe they are capable of learning math.
	Students feel socially tied to peers, faculty, and the course.
	Students believe the course has value.
	Students have skills, habits and know-how to succeed in college setting.
	Faculty and college support students' skills and mindsets.

Note. Retrieved from https://www.carnegiefoundation.org/in-action/carnegie-math-pathways/ productive-persistence/

the Productive Persistence framework). The students who had failed the college math placement test had to take the remedial math course, and many of these students needed to be convinced that they were "capable of learning math" (Beattie, 2015). This component is a factor that must not be overlooked because "students' beliefs about themselves as learners and the nature of learning have a marked influence on motivation" (Richlin, 2006, p. 116).

To assist in implementing the first component, the professors attended Productive Persistence workshops, where they discussed and practiced positive ways they could encourage their students to adopt a growth mindset. In their courses, students did not just hear about the growth mindset, they read about it. As mentioned in chapter 4, students read a short article about how intelligence can grow titled "You Can Grow Your Brain: New Research Shows the Brain Can Be Developed Like a Muscle," by Blackwell (2002). (See chapter 4 for further discussion on mindsets.) After reading the article, professors had short class discussions with their students. Another part of the first component included promoting sustained effort and help-seeking behaviors (Beattie, 2015).

Yeager and Dweck (2012) performed a study in which they introduced college students to the incremental theory of intelligence and growth mindsets. They found that the positive effects "of learning that intelligence is improvable were slightly greater for African American students, who may face greater challenges in college than White students because of negative stereotypes about their group's intellectual ability" (p. 204). Additionally, Bean and Eaton (2001–2002) note that of the psychological processes that play into students' successful academic integration in higher education, one of the most important is the "self-efficacy assessment [where students are asking,]

'Do I have confidence that I can perform well academically here?'" (p. 75). When we have discussions with our students about growing intelligence and having a growth mindset, we are also letting them know that we believe they can perform well.

I have worked with students (many who were minority, first-generation, and/or academically unprepared) who shared with me their doubts about their own abilities to learn. The following incident is an example of how students' self-doubt can hinder the actions that we, their professors, expect out of our students—coming to our office hours for help. I have always stressed the importance of students going to see their professors during office hours so they could ask questions and clarify course material they were confused about. Still, many did not follow my advice. When Isaiah, an African American, first-generation, low-income student, was talking to me about one of his classes taught by another professor, I said to him, "Oh, I know that teacher. He's really nice. Come on, I'll walk with you over to his office." As we were walking across campus, Isaiah was visibly nervous. I asked what was troubling him. He told me, "I'm not sure I want to talk to Dr. Z because he'll find out that I'm stupid and not good enough to be here." It was such a surprise to hear this because I knew this young man was extremely capable and only lacked the experience and preparation to be ready for college. The meeting with his professor did take place, and, between the two of us, we were able to share with Isaiah our confidence in him. We had a tremendous impact on his motivation and the effort that he put forth in both of our classes. This kind of intervention works well for many other students who have similar backgrounds and doubts about their capabilities to learn.

The second component of implementing the Productive Persistence program was to help students feel socially tied to peers—or fellow classmates—and to the faculty member who was teaching the course section they were taking. Students were interviewed about their feelings of not belonging, and professors had discussions with students about perceived negative or low expectations (Beattie, 2015). Of course, the purpose of the discussions was to counter such perceptions. Faculty spent time building relationships with their students and invited upperclassmen who had been successful to come to classes to talk to the lowerclassmen (Beattie, 2015). In addition to increased retention, student involvement with academics, faculty, and peers "powerfully influences degree attainment" (Astin & Oseguera, 2012, p. 124). As discussed in chapter 2, learning our students' names is a first step to creating a class climate where students feel they belong, and we can also help students learn each other's names. Having peer and faculty interactions during class has many benefits. As P. Talbert (2012) notes, "Peer interactions and associations influence students' cognitive development, self-confidence, and motivation" (p. 23). Most students from *all* backgrounds appreciate professors and classmates who take a personal interest in them.

One major goal of the Productive Persistence project was for students to recognize that they are a part of the community of learners. Johnson and colleagues (2007) found that "students have a fundamental need to feel that they are an important part of a larger community that is valuable, supportive, and affirming" (p. 527). Fleming (2012) and M. N. Thompson (2013) also highlighted the importance of *being connected* and having *feelings of belonging* for minority students, and the positive impact of these two factors on retention and persistence. Providing opportunities for students to work together on academic tasks can also create connections among the students and promote a learning community. (Throughout this book, many meaningful educational activities have been suggested; additionally, many colleges and universities have faculty development programs that can give professors specific assistance.)

Another way professors helped students feel socially tied to the course was having open discussions about trust and using corrective feedback as a vehicle for building trust. The feedback included one component in which students were provided specific information on what they were doing right and a second component in which specific corrective feedback was given on what they needed to do to improve. By showing students where they needed to improve and by giving them strategies they could use, the message from the professors was that they believed in the students' ability to grow and improve. This kind of feedback also supports the growth mindset of believing in the incremental theory of intelligence.

Yeager and Dweck's (2012) findings support using this kind of feedback. They agree that when professors focused on the "process" (e.g., you need a better strategy) rather than on "ability" (you're just not good at math), students viewed their teachers as having higher expectations for them, and this helped the students "respond to challenges resiliently" (Yeager & Dweck, p. 311). A major aspect of the feedback process was allowing students to resubmit their work for a higher grade once they had received feedback from their professors. (See chapter 7 for further discussion on resubmitting work.) More than just allowing the resubmit practice, it was expected that the students would make corrections and resubmit. "Setting high expectations and then supporting and holding students accountable for reaching them is an effective strategy for encouraging student success" (Kuh et al., 2006, p. 67).

A third component of the Productive Persistence program was to help students see the value in the course. The professors spent time in class identifying the relevance of the course content, and they also had the students think and write about the benefits of the course. Incorporating this component in all of our classes, no matter the subject or department, can be extremely beneficial. To accomplish this, we can begin by stating clear course objectives in our course syllabus and including the "promises or opportunities" the course offers to the students (Bain, 2004, p. 75).

Next, we must show how our course has relevance to our students' academic lives and to their future professional lives. We can also emphasize real-world applications that relate to the content (and skills) that our course will cover (Eberly Center, 2015; Grunert O'Brien et al., 2008). We can lay out our vision of the value of our course, but we can also ask our students to reflect on and contribute to the relevancy of the course. Doing so can enhance their motivation, engagement, and learning because "students will be more motivated to work hard if they see the value of what they are learning to their overall course of study . . . [and] if they anticipate an eventual payoff in terms of their future professional lives" (Eberly Center, 2015, p. 1). (See chapters 3 and 5 for further discussion on relevancy.)

The fourth component of the Productive Persistence program was helping students develop the skills, habits, and know-how to succeed in the college setting. This included emotional regulation, stress reappraisal, and use of metacognitive strategies that would lead to longer retention of information. When examining the ways to enhance the retention and academic performance of minority students, Fleming (2012) points out that possessing organizational know-how is necessary for success as well as "knowing how to manage the college environments" (p. 5). In many of our courses, we can help students understand how the skills they are developing in our class can be used in other college courses.

The skills, habits, and know-how to succeed also emphasize relevance of the course as it relates to the students' academic lives. For example, the math course included lessons on how to fill out financial aid forms, which is also an aspect of knowing how to succeed in college. For two courses that I teach in the education department, I include lessons on how to write and use e-mails in a professional manner. The two main sources I used for the lessons are Email Etiquette for Students and Email Etiquette Dos & Don'ts.[1] The e-mail skills are ones students need while in college, but they can also be useful in their personal and professional lives.

The fifth and final component for implementing the Productive Persistence program was faculty and college support for students' skills and growth mindsets (Beattie, 2015). This component included faculty development. The professors were a major part in developing the components of Productive Persistence, and they had workshops on effective ways to implement each part. For example, to implement the different components, professors had short 20-minute sessions for a total of about six hours. The

Carnegie Foundation for the Advancement of Teaching (n.d.) explains why faculty development is so important:

> A key component of institutional responsibility lies in the area of professional development. If faculty are to implement and sustain more effective approaches in their classrooms—and to continue to improve upon them—campuses must reinvent professional development as an intellectually engaging, integral element of their ongoing work.

The community colleges that participated in the Productive Persistence project had tremendous success. In developmental mathematics courses, after one month, the probability of course success increased from 60% to 90%. The number of students dropping out of the developmental mathematics courses decreased by 51% (Carnegie Foundation for the Advancement of Teaching, n.d.).

While Tinto's (2006–2007) model includes explicit connections to both the academic and social environments of the college, struggling and unprepared students' connections to academics are usually the ultimate determinant of their retention and success rates. Without passing classes, and in most cases without maintaining at least the required minimum grade point average, students cannot remain enrolled. Students' ability to pass the remedial math class is an important factor for retention, persistence, and graduation. Math has been a major hurdle for many community college students, and failing this requirement can keep them from graduating (Grunder & Hellmich, 1996). Thus, the results of the Productive Persistence project have been far reaching.

Tinto (2012) points out that "for students who enter college academically underprepared or who have struggled academically in the past, success depends as much on their coming to see themselves as being able to succeed as it does the acquisition of basic skills" (p. 27). In addition to unprepared students, Tinto notes that this situation is also true for many minority, low-income, and first-generation students. The "importance of validation of success of underserved students" can make a difference in these students' "likelihood of subsequent success" (Tinto, 2012, p. 27).

Conclusion

Engstrom (2008) points out that "the number of students attending colleges and universities has increased over 25 percent in the past twenty years . . . . Daunting challenges still remain to improve the completion of baccalaureate degrees, particularly for those who come unprepared" (p. 5). In addition to the academically unprepared students, minority and first-generation students are having trouble staying in college and earning their degree.

An institution cannot respond to *all* of the needs of *all* of our students. Nonetheless, as professors, we can certainly help many students improve and succeed through the methods we implement in our classrooms. Laird and colleagues (2008) note that "if faculty members use principles of good practice to design assignments and engaging pedagogies to structure in-class and out-of-class activities, students would ostensibly put forth more effort" (p. 87). At each college and university, and within each department, professors must respond to the needs of their students within the context of their subject, content, and particular environment. We know that there is no "one-size-fits-all" solution to improving retention, persistence, and graduation rates at different colleges and universities (Seidman, 2012).

Still, by what we do and how we teach, professors can impact "multiple forms of student success . . . [, including] academic attainment, acquisition of a general education, development of academic competence, development of cognitive skills and intellectual dispositions, occupational attainment, and preparation for adulthood and citizenship" (Braxton, 2008, p. 103). Earning a college degree goes beyond passing tests or earning good grades. As Rendon (2006) notes, when considering the characteristics of "educated students," we also consider characteristics such as how to be "good humanitarians, get along with others, have a sense of purpose, work effectively with diversity, and develop values related to democracy and social justice" (p. 15).

As our students enter our colleges and universities, I believe that professors can be instrumental in increasing their chances of leaving with a completed course of study and a degree that signifies their acquired knowledge and ability to learn, as well as with an appreciation for lifelong learning and a willingness to actively participate as educated citizens in our democratic society.

Note

1. See https://owl.english.purdue.edu/owl/resource/694/01/ and www.emilypost.com/communication-and-technology/computers-and-communication/459-email-etiquette-dos-and-donts

FINAL THOUGHTS

Teacher Impact on Diverse College Students

As I traveled across the country conducting workshops and presentations based on my previous book, *Teaching Unprepared Students: Strategies for Promoting Success and Retention in Higher Education* (Gabriel, 2008), many professors and administrators would inquire about students who were dropping out early or not performing in their classes although these students were not academically unprepared. We had many discussions regarding students who traditionally have had low retention, success, and graduation rates, particularly minority students and first-generation students, and it is from those discussions and inquiries that this book was inspired. It is intended as a continuation of my first book, and its purpose is to examine additional methods and techniques that have proven to have an impact on student learning and success. I want to emphasize again that I do not have all the answers and that neither book is a panacea for the many challenges that we face as professors. Nevertheless, I hope that the methods, ideas, and concepts presented here will assist professors as they seek to increase the success of *all* students in their courses, especially those who have traditionally been underserved.

Furthermore, I hope the contents of this book will contribute to and generate discussions as we think about our teaching and the impact that we can have on our students. Although good grades and passing our classes are important metrics, they do not always reflect deep learning and a real understanding of core concepts. We need to facilitate that as well as develop our students' growth in their own knowledge, critical thinking skills, communication skills (both speaking and writing), problem-solving skills, and so on, which increase our students' intellectual efficacy (Bandura, 1994). We should always keep high expectations for our students, and at the same time provide support and guidance to help them reach those expectations, with the full awareness that we will not be able to help or reach everyone. However, let us guard against making assumptions prematurely, and against our own biases, hidden or exposed, about whom we will or will not be able to reach. Let us also purposefully work to develop a class climate that is inviting and accepting for all of our diverse students.

We live in a complex world, and as our students leave colleges and universities to become active citizens in our democratic society, their education matters—it matters not only for the kind of career or profession they are pursuing but also in their readiness to be involved in civic duties and activities. Astin (1999a) points out the following:

> In a democracy . . . citizen disengagement from politics and governmental ineffectiveness not only go hand in hand, but also cripple our capacity to deal constructively with most of the other problems . . . [such as] shaky race relations, growing economic disparities and inequities, excessive materialism, decaying inner cities, a deteriorating infrastructure, a weakening public school system, . . . [and] declining civic 'engagement' to name a few. (p. 8)

Furthermore, Astin (1999a) reminds us, as professors and teachers at colleges and universities, we must shoulder "some of the responsibility for solving these problems" (p. 8). I believe, as the teaching faculty, we should be aware of the impact we can have on our students in assisting them in their awareness and sense of civic responsibilities.

We are not alone in this mission. There are also many resources on campuses for our students such as "academic advisers, librarians, and retention specialists . . . counselors and tutors" (Gabriel, 2008, p. 119), to name a few. As professors, we can also receive support and help from multicultural, teaching, or faculty development centers that are on our campuses. However, let me be clear: We must be major players in the efforts to improve graduation rates for all of our students.

Finally, I would like to conclude on a personal note by thanking the many professors and teachers whom I have met and worked with throughout my teaching career. Many have inspired me in their work. As I noted in my previous book (Gabriel, 2008), to be effective teachers, we "need to have genuine enthusiasm for teaching and a sincere interest in *all* of our students' learning" (p. 120). I hope that the techniques and teaching methods discussed in this book will support the passion that you have for teaching and the positive impact that you have on your students.

Readings for Expanding Cultural Competence

The following books and online program are not meant to be an exhaustive list of resources; they are some of my favorite books that helped me expand my cultural competence and awareness. If you have recommendations, please e-mail them to me at kgabriel@u.arizona.edu. Thank you!

Nonfiction Books and Articles

Angelou, M. (1969). *I know why the caged bird sings.* New York, NY: Bantam Books.

Bennett, L. (1982). *Before the Mayflower: A history of black America* (5th ed.). New York, NY: Penguin Books.

Brown, D. (1970). *Bury my heart at Wounded Knee: An Indian history of the American west.* New York, NY: Bantam Books.

Burciaga, J. (1992). *Drink cultura: Chicanism.* Santa Barbara, CA: Joshua Odell Editions.

Coates, T.-N. (2014, June). The case for reparations. *Atlantic, 313*(5), 54–71. Retrieved from https://www.theatlantic.com/magazine/archive/2014/06/the-case-for-reparations/361631/

Coates, T.-N. (2015). *Between the world and me: The beautiful struggle.* New York, NY: Spiegel & Grau.

Conrat, M., & Conrat, R. (1972). *Executive order 9066: The internment of 110,000 Japanese Americans.* California Historical Society. Los Angeles, CA: Anderson, Ritchie & Simon.

Crow Dog, M., & Erdoes, R. (1990). *Lakota woman.* New York, NY: Harper Perennial.

Douglass, F. (1982). *Narrative of the life of Frederick Douglass, an American slave* (H. Baker, Ed.). New York, NY: Penguin Books.

Du Bois, W. E. B. (1903). *The souls of black folks.* New York, NY: Penguin Books.

Howard, T. (2014). *Black male(d): Peril and promise in the education of African American males.* New York, NY: Teachers College Press.

Jacobs, H. A. (1987). *Incidents in the life of a slave girl* (J. F. Yellin, Ed.). Cambridge, MA: Harvard University Press.

Jones, L., & Newman, L. (with Isay, D.). (1997). *Our America: Life and death on the south side of Chicago*. New York, NY: Pocket Books.

Kozol, J. (1991). *Salvage inequalities: Children in America's schools*. New York, NY: Harper Perennial.

Lanker, B. (1989). *I dream a world: Portraits of Black women who changed America*. New York, NY: Stewart, Tabori & Chang.

Moody, A. (1968). *Coming of age in Mississippi*. New York, NY: Doubleday.

Moore, J. (1991). *Going down to the barrio: Homeboys and homegirls in change*. Philadelphia, PA: Temple University Press.

Salley, C. (1999). *The Black 100: A ranking of the most influential African-Americans, past and present*. New York, NY: Citadel Press.

Tatum, B. D. (1997). *"Why are all the Black kids sitting together in the cafeteria?" And other conversations about race*. New York, NY: Basic Books.

Voss, F. S. (1995). *Majestic in his wrath: A pictorial life of Frederick Douglass*. Washington, DC: Smithsonian Institution Press.

Watson, L. W., Terrell, M. C., Wright, D. J., Bonner, F. A. II, Cuyjet, M. J., Gold, J. A., . . . Person, D. R. (2002). *How minority students experience college: Implications for planning and policy*. Sterling, VA: Stylus.

Wells, I. B. (1970). *Crusade for justice: The autobiography of Ida B. Wells* (A. M. Duster, Ed.). Chicago, IL: The University of Chicago Press.

West, C. (1993). *Race matters*. New York, NY: Vintage Books.

Wright, R. (1945). *Black boy*. New York, NY: Buccaneer Books.

Fiction Books

Anaya, R. (1972). *Bless me, Ultima*. Berkeley, CA: Tonatiuh-Quinto Sol (TQS) International.

Cisneros, S. (1989). *The House on Mango Street*. New York, NY: Vintage Books. (This book is a combination of fiction, poetry, and autobiography.)

Halley, A. (1976). *Roots: The saga of an American family*. New York, NY: Dell.

Hansberry, L. (1959). *A raisin in the sun*. New York, NY: Vintage Books. (Recently, the play was on Broadway again, starring Denzel Washington. The first movie based on this book, starring Sidney Poitier and Ruby Dee, is fabulous. You can watch it on YouTube.)

Hurston, Z. N. (1937). *Their eyes were watching God*. Greenwich, CT: Fawcett Premier Books.

Lee, H. (1960). *To kill a mockingbird*. New York, NY: HarperCollins. (You may have read this book in your youth, but I recommend reading it again as an adult.)

Morrison, T. (1977). *Song of Solomon*. New York, NY: First Signet Printing.

Simmen, E. (Ed.). (1971). *The Chicano: From caricature to self-portrait*. New York, NY: Signet. (This book contains stories and self-portraits, so it could be classified as both fiction and nonfiction.)

Welch, J. (1974). *Winter in the blood*. New York, NY: Penguin Books.

Welch, J. (1986). *Fools crow*. New York, NY: Penguin Classics.

Welch, J. (1990). *The Indian lawyer*. New York, NY: Penguin Books.

Wilson, A. (1986). *Fences*. New York, NY: Penguin Books. (Pulitzer Prize winner)

Wilson, A. (1990). *The piano lesson*. New York, NY: Penguin Books. (Pulitzer Prize winner)

Wright, R. (1940). *Native son*. New York, NY: Harper.

Online Program

Adelman, L., series executive producer and codirector of California Newsreel. (2003, April). PBS.org. *Race: The power of an illusion*. Available at http://www.pbs.org/race/001_WhatIsRace/001_00-home.htm

Organizing Student Interaction With
Multiple Small-Group Configurations

This appendix originally appeared in Kathleen F. Gabriel's (2008) book, *Teaching Unprepared Students: Strategies for Promoting Success and Retention in Higher Education* (pp. 127–130). It is reproduced here with permission.

TABLE B.1
Sample "Groupings" for a Class of 33 Students

Number	Color	Time	Student's Name
5	BLUE	10 AM	
1	GREEN	10 AM	
4	ORANGE	10 AM	
7	YELLOW	10 AM	
2	BLACK	12 NOON	
4	BROWN	12 NOON	
3	RED	12 NOON	
7	VIOLET	12 NOON	
8	BLACK	3 PM	
6	BLUE	3 PM	
9	PINK	3 PM	
6	BROWN	4 PM	
2	GREEN	4 PM	
3	PINK	4 PM	
4	YELLOW	4 PM	
1	RED	5 AM	
3	GREEN	5 PM	

(Continues)

Table B.1 (*Continued*)

Number	Color	Time	Student's Name
8	PINK	5 PM	
5	YELLOW	5 PM	
1	PURPLE	6 AM	
9	TURQUOISE	6 AM	
8	VIOLET	6 AM	
9	BROWN	7 PM	
6	ORANGE	7 PM	
2	RED	7 PM	
1	BLUE	8 AM	
5	ORANGE	8 AM	
3	PURPLE	8 AM	
6	TURQUOISE	8 AM	
4	BLACK	9 AM	
7	PURPLE	9 AM	
5	TURQUOISE	9 AM	
2	VIOLET	9 AM	

Grouping Strategy

Divide your class into three different groups using numbers, colors, and time of day. To do this, first adjust the list in Table B.1 to fit the size of your class. If you want each group size to be 3 students, or if you have more or less than 33 students, add or subtract from the list. You can use the "sort tool key" to rearrange the chart by categories (e.g., you can sort the "color" column so that all of the colors—i.e., all reds, all pinks, all yellows, etc.—are together).

Once you have adjusted the preceding list for a specific class, make up an index card for each line on your adjusted list. (See example card in Figure B.1.) Then, before class, shuffle the cards. As students come into class, have each student draw one of the cards, or after they have taken a seat, go around the room and give students a card.

After the cards are distributed, each student will write his or her name on the card and turn it back into you. From the random card drawing, you can create a master list for each grouping. Then, when students get into a

Figure B.1. Sample three-inch-by-five-inch card.

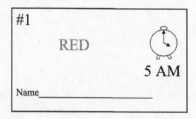

group, you can announce whether they are to get into their "number" group, or "color" group, or "time of day" group. By having three different group possibilities, students will have the opportunity to meet and work with lots of other students in the class.

NOTE: Another way that I assign students to the small-group configuration is to put the information on the back of the students' nameplates as described in chapter 2.

Quote of the Week: Examples From Diverse People for Supporting Growth Mindsets and Mental Toughness Attributes

I n this appendix I provide additional examples of quotes that I use to expose students to successful individuals who initially faced obstacles and failures and to share real-world examples of growth mindsets (see Figure C.1 for PowerPoint slide examples). The Quote of the Week is intended to reinforce a positive growth mindset and mental toughness attributes. (See chapter 4.)

Figure C.1. Examples of Quote of the Week in PowerPoint slides.

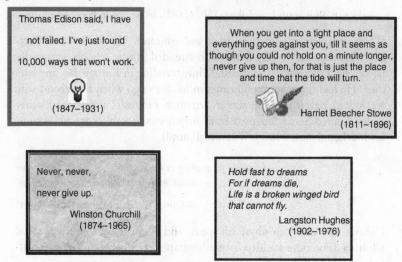

Note. From Edison (n.d.); Stowe (n.d.); Churchill (n.d.); Hughes (n.d.).

Additional Quotes for Inspiration

> *Always bear in mind that your own resolution to*
> *succeed is more important than any other.*

—Abraham Lincoln (1809–1865)

> *Do not let what you cannot do interfere with what you can do.*

—John Wooden (1910–2010)

> *Success is peace of mind which is a direct result of self-satisfaction in know-*
> *ing you did your best to become the best you are capable of becoming.*

—Coach John Wooden (1910–2010)

Wooden was an American basketball and head coach at the University of California, Los Angeles; he coached his college basketball team to 10 National Championships. Also, he is author of several books and created the "Pyramid of Success" model of what it takes to succeed.

> *Perseverance is a great element of success. If you only knock long enough*
> *and loud enough at the gate, you are sure to wake up somebody.*

—Henry Wadsworth Longfellow (1807–1882), an American poet and educator

Wadsworth was an American poet and educator. He was born in Portland, Maine, to a wealthy family and attended private schools, eventually becoming a professor at Harvard. While traveling in Europe, his first wife died. He had other sorrowful times in his life (e.g., when his second wife was killed); nevertheless, he was an extremely successful and popular writer in the United States (adapted from http://www.notablebiographies.com/Lo-Ma/Longfellow-Henry-Wadsworth.html).

> *I find the great thing in this world is not so much where we*
> *stand, as in what direction we are moving.*

—Oliver Wendell Holmes (1809–1894)

Holmes, an American physician, poet, and scientist, was also a medical reformer. (For more see http://www.biography.com/people/oliver-wendell-holmes-9342379.)

> *What we obtain too cheap, we esteem too lightly.*

—Thomas Paine (1737–1809)

Paine was an inventor and writer. He is the author of *Common Sense* and other writings that influenced the American Revolution (see https://www .biography.com/people/thomas-paine-9431951 for more).

> *The mere imparting of information is not education. Above all things, the effort must result in making a man think and do for himself.*
>
> —Carter G. Woodson (1875–1950)

Known as the "Father of Black History Month," Woodson was an African American writer and historian. As a child, he worked as a sharecropper and miner to help his family. When he started high school, he completed a four-year course of study in only two years, and as he continued in his education he eventually earned a PhD from Harvard University (see https:// www.biography.com/people/carter-g-woodson-9536515 for more).

> *Education remains the key to both economic and political empowerment.*
>
> —Barbara Jordan (1936–1991)

Jordan was elected to the Texas Senate in 1966; she was the first Black senator elected to that office since 1883. She also served three highly visible terms in the U.S. House of Representatives. She grew up in a poor Black neighborhood in Houston, Texas. By the time she was in high school, she was working hard to obtain academic excellence. She went to college and became a lawyer before entering politics (see https://www.biography.com/ people/barbara-jordan-9357991 for more).

> *Education is not preparation for life. Education is life itself.*
>
> —John Dewey (1859–1952)

Dewey was an American educational reformer, psychologist, and philosopher. See https://www.pbs.org/onlyateacher/john.html for his work and influence in the field of education. Dewey believed that "learning by doing and development of practical life skills" should be a crucial component of children's education.

> *Determination and perseverance move the world; thinking that others will do it for you is a sure way to fail.*
>
> —Marva Collins (1936–2015)

> *When someone is taught the joy of learning, it becomes a life-long process that never stops, a process that creates a logical individual. That is the challenge and joy of teaching.*
>
> —Marva Collins (1936–2015)

Marva Collins was an American educator who started Westside Preparatory School in the impoverished Garfield Park neighborhood of Chicago in 1975. She was born in Monroeville, Alabama, and was raised in a segregated south where she had to attend poor, inadequate schools. Libraries in the south were for "Whites only." After she married, she was a substitute teacher for 14 years, during which she witnessed firsthand the poor quality of public schools on the West Side of Chicago. She decided to start her own school (private but with a low tuition) so that African American students would have equal access to a top-quality education. She had high expectations for all her students (adapted from https://www.biography.com/people/marva-collins-5894).

> *We should seek not a world where the black race and white race live in harmony, but a world in which the terms black and white have no real political meaning.*

—Ta-Nehisi Coates (1975–)

Coates is an American author and journalist who addresses cultural, social, and political issues. He has won several literary awards for his articles in *Atlantic* magazine, and his book *Between the World and Me* (2015) is a best seller. (See his book and one of his articles listed in Appendix A.)

> *Once social change begins, it cannot be reversed. You cannot un-educate the person who has learned to read. You cannot humiliate the person who feels pride. You cannot oppress the people who are not afraid anymore.*

—Cesar Chavez (1927–1993)

> *To make a great dream come true, the first requirement is a great capacity to dream; the second is persistence.*

—Cesar Chavez (1927–1993)

> *History will judge societies and governments—and their institutions—not by how big they are or how well they serve the rich and the powerful, but by how effectively they respond to the needs of the poor and the helpless.*

—Cesar Chavez (1927–1993)

> *Preservation of one's own culture does not require contempt or disrespect for other cultures.*

—Cesar Chavez (1927–1993)

> *Grant me courage to serve others; For in service there is true life. . . . In giving of yourself, you will discover a whole new life full of meaning and love.*

—Cesar Chavez (1927–1993)

Chavez was an American labor leader and civil rights activist. He was born in Arizona, where as a young child he and his family were migrant farmworkers. So, he knew firsthand the horrible pay and working conditions these workers endured. When he grew up, he founded the National Farm Workers Association and in 1965 organized the first ever strike in California against grape growers. He worked to improve the working conditions of the farmworkers using nonviolent means to bring attention to the horrible conditions they faced. Because of Mr. Chavez, many changes were brought about (adapted from https://www.biography.com/people/cesar-chavez-9245781).

A battle lost or won is easily described, understood, and appreciated, but the moral growth of a great nation requires reflection, as well as observation, to appreciate it.

—Frederick Douglass (ca. 1818–1895)

No man can put a chain about the ankle of his fellow man without at last finding the other end fastened about his own neck.

—Frederick Douglass (ca. 1818–1895)

Though conscious of the difficulty of learning without a teacher, I set out with high hope, and a fixed purpose, at whatever cost or trouble, to learn how to read.

—Frederick Douglass (ca. 1818–1895)

Without education he lives within the narrow, dark and grimy walls of ignorance. Education, on the other hand, means emancipation. It means light and liberty. It means the uplifting of the soul of man into the glorious light of truth, the light by which men can only be made free. To deny education to any people is one of the greatest crimes against human nature. It is easy to deny them the means of freedom and the rightful pursuit of happiness and to defeat the very end of their being.

—Frederick Douglass (ca. 1818–1895)

Douglass was born into slavery, but he was able to escape when he was about 20 years old. He then became famous as an antislavery activist. His writings and his speeches are considered American classics. He also worked to abolish "Jim Crow" and lynchings in the 1890s. (For more information, see http://www.history.com/topics/black-history/frederick-douglass; also see his book listed in Appendix A.)

You can pray until you faint, but unless you get up and try to do something, God is not going to put it in your lap.

—Fannie Lou Hamer (1917–1977)

Hamer, a civil rights activist and philanthropist, was the youngest of 20 children. Her parents were sharecroppers in the Mississippi Delta area. Hamer worked the fields at an early age. Her family struggled financially and often went hungry. As an adult, she worked for desegregation and voter rights— or voter registration! As a civil rights activist, she was arrested and beaten by the police. See http://www.pbs.org/wgbh/americanexperience/features/ freedomsummer-hamer/ for more of her works. Also watch https://www .youtube.com/watch?v=07PwNVCZCcY for her oral testimony.

> *Don't be afraid of the space between your dreams and reality.*
> *If you can dream it, you can make it so.*

—Belva Davis (1932–)

Davis is an American television and radio journalist. She grew up in Oakland, California, and began writing freelance articles for magazines in 1957. As the first Black female TV journalist on the West Coast, she helped change the face and focus of TV news. She has won eight Emmy Awards and has been recognized by the American Women in Radio and Television and by the National Association of Black Journalists (http:// www.belvadavis.com/about). In her book, *Never in My Wildest Dreams*, she tells about her many struggles, challenges, and determination to succeed.

> *Education is the most powerful weapon which we can use to change the world.*

—Nelson Mandela (1918–2013)

Mandela was a politician, philanthropist, and antiapartheid revolutionary from South Africa. He served as president of South Africa from 1994 to 1999 (see https://www.nelsonmandela.org/content/page/biography for more).

> *I have learned that success is to be measured not so much by the position that one has reached in life as by the obstacles which he has had to overcome while trying to succeed.*

—Booker T. Washington (1856–1915)

Washington was born into slavery. Once free, he became an educator and rose to be one of the most influential African Americans of his time. He founded the Tuskegee Institute in Alabama for training teachers (see http:// www.history.com/topics/black-history/booker-t-washington fore more).

To find additional quotes, you can use online resources such as http:// thinkexist.com or www.inspirational-quotes.info. There are also numerous quote books at most bookstores.

Note-Taking Tips for Students and a Few Tips for Professors

Gabriel's Top 10 Tips for Better Note Taking

1. Use standard 8.5-inch-by-11-inch loose-leaf lined paper (already hole punched) that you can file in a 3-ring binder. Use tabs so you can create specific sections for each class. This will also allow you to punch holes in any handouts provided with a specific class. "Spiral notebooks do not allow reshuffling of notes for review" (Academic Skills Center, n.d.).

2. Put a pencil/pen "pocket holder" in the front of your binder, where you can keep extra pencils or pens and even a handheld hole puncher. This might seem "uncool," but it will come in handy many times during the semester.

3. Start each class by entering the day and date first at the top of your notebook paper. This will help you when cross-referencing notes with readings and reviewing for tests and/or assignments. Also, for any assignments given in class, put a space between your class notes and the assignment, and even draw a box around or highlight the assignment. Borrow, or develop, your own system for indenting, numbering, and showing emphasis (e.g., with an asterisk or special symbol).

4. Only write on one side of the paper. It will help with your organization.

5. When professors give examples, put those in your notes in abbreviated form and later add your own example. These examples can make a big difference in your overall comprehension and recall.

6. "**BE SYSTEMATIC**—so you can establish a habit and pattern so you won't miss anything important" (Academic Skills Center, n.d.). This means not missing class and, moreover, getting to class a few minutes ahead of time so you can be set up and ready to pay attention as soon as class begins. It also means noting the way the lecture is organized, especially in the way the teacher presents information/concepts.

7. Write—do not type. You do not need to be a "court reporter" taking down word for word what is on the PowerPoints, or what the professor

is saying. Listen for key points, and as you write, feel free to use your own words; this will help you pay attention and process what is being covered. Then, during a pause or break, go back and add what else you remember. (It is okay to compare notes with a classmate and even visit your professor during office hours to clarify so you can add to your notes.) NOTE: If you like to write exactly what a teacher says, that is fine, but be sure to translate or paraphrase it at some point. Several research studies show that by writing your own notes you can synthesize, paraphrase, and summarize the content much better, and, as a result, your comprehension and retention will be greatly improved.

8. Most important: "Make notes as complete as needed and as clear as possible so they can be used meaningfully later" (Academic Skills Center, n.d.).

9. "Leave blanks where information is missed or not understood. Fill in gaps after lecture or as soon after as possible with the aid of the instructor or classmates" (Academic Skills Center, n.d.).

10. Keep in mind that it is okay to use a lot of paper when taking notes. Do not give up even if you have trouble at the beginning of the semester. Remember, you will get better at note taking the more you do it.

Summary of Tips for Professors (or How to Help Students With Note Taking)

1. Start off the semester by sharing with students the importance of taking notes and some of the research supporting handwritten notes. Hand out the previous list of tips or create your own. Reminding students again after the first midterm or middle of the semester can also be beneficial. Many students falsely believe that taking notes will distract them from listening or that material the professor is covering is in the readings or handouts. Some students are not aware that they should be taking notes (Bligh, 2000).

2. In addition to the research presented in chapter 5 by Cornelius and Owen-DeSchryver (2008), also remind students why they should take notes by hand rather than using a laptop. In their study, Mueller and Oppenheimer (2014) found that students who took notes with a pen (as opposed to those who used a laptop) had a better grasp of the material. In fact, they concluded that using laptops for note taking can have a negative effect on students' performance. When students took notes by hand, they did more "synthesizing and summarizing [of] content rather

than verbatim transcription[, which served] . . . as a desirable difficulty toward improved educational outcomes" (Mueller & Oppenheimer, 2014, p. 1166).

3. Keep in mind that although it is not a good idea to give out complete notes to students, giving out a handout of a skeleton or brief outline of the lecture can be helpful especially for first- and second-year students. (This goes for PowerPoint handouts as well.) When you do this, announce to students that they must "fill in" the details of what is being presented and discussed in class; remind them that doing so will help them remember, and it can also help them stay engaged, as noted in chapter 5.

4. Do not talk too fast and be sure to pause for at least one or two minutes after covering a portion of content and ask students to look over their notes (Weimer, 2013). This will also give students time to add in information and reflect on what has been covered so far, as mentioned in chapter 5.

5. Give clear signals for key points that need to be written down. For example, say, "This is important so write it down" or "There are three key important points . . . ," (as mentioned in chapter 5).

6. Consider allowing use of notes, or a "limited use of notes" during exams (or during quizzes), which can motivate students to improve their note taking (Weimer, 2013). For example, announce to students that they will be able to use their class notes and handouts on the quiz that you will give at the next class (or next week's class.)

A Strategy for Building Vocabulary

The Vocabulary Strategy Steps: Instructions for the Students

The steps described in this section are from Kathleen Gabriel's *Learn the Lingo: A Strategy for Building a Better Vocabulary, Student Booklet, Volume I* (1999a) and *Learn the Lingo: A Strategy for Building a Better Vocabulary, Teacher's Manual* (1999b). (Teacher's Manual, Volumes 1 and 2, with 10 lessons and quizzes for each and Student Booklet, Volume 2 are also available. Send requests to kgabriel@u.arizona.edu.) Reprinted here with permission.

STEP 1: Write the vocabulary word (or bold printed word from your textbook) in the center of a three-inch-by-five-inch card that has holes punched on the top. The punched holes should be the same width as binder rings so the card can easily be clipped into your binder (see Figure D.1). You should write the word neatly and in a normal size print or cursive. (Large block print should not be used). Use your normal handwriting because that will assist in the brain-hand linkage

Figure D.1. The front of a vocabulary card.

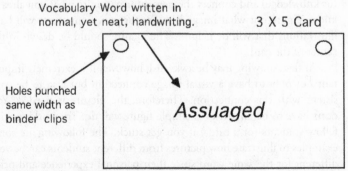

Note. The front should only have the vocabulary word written on it. No other information should appear on the front.

Figure D.2. The back of a vocabulary card.

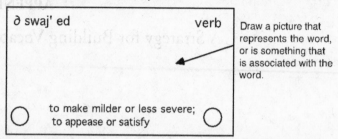

Note. Information is written on the top and bottom of the card so that there is room in the middle for your drawing.

and in memory retention. *Example*: assuaged (from the first page of the novel, *To Kill a Mockingbird*, [Lee, 1960]).

STEP 2: Flip the card over so that the holes are now on the bottom. For a new vocabulary word, write the word's part-of-speech in the upper right-hand corner of the card (see Figure D.2). For a word from a textbook, write the chapter number and/or page number that the bold printed word is on.

STEP 3: Next, if needed, write the word's pronunciation guide in the upper left-hand corner of the card. This step is optional. (See Figure D.2.)

STEP 4: Write the word's definition on the bottom of the card, leaving the middle part empty. Look up unknown words and break down the definition until it makes sense. If you are using a textbook, avoid using the textbook's glossary. Instead read through the paragraph that the word is embedded in.

STEP 5: This is the most important step in making the card. Think of an image that connects or links the definition to the word and then draw a picture representing that image. Think about your prior experience (or knowledge) and connect the new information to what you already know. Figure out what image best fits for you. Some texts will have illustrations that will be helpful. The picture should be drawn in the center of the card.

At first, drawing may be awkward; however, it is extremely important not only to have a visual image connection but also to be consistent with this connection. Therefore, the picture is needed. You don't have to be an artist—a simple figure will do. Try working with fellow students (or a tutor) if you get stuck. The following are some examples to illustrate how pictures from different students can be very different for the same word since their personal experience and prior knowledge are different (See Figure D.3).

Figure D.3. Examples of different drawings for the same word.

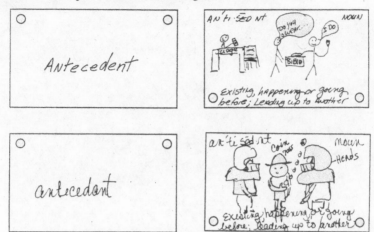

Note. In the drawing on top, the student draws a person having swearing in *before* testifying in court; in the drawing on the bottom, the student draws the coin toss which happens *before* a football game starts.

Self-Test Using Your Vocabulary Cards

After you have made your own vocabulary cards, there are different ways to "self-test." For example, lay out all the cards with the word on the front face up. Then, pick out one card and say the definition without looking on the back. After you say the answer to yourself, look at the answer on the back of the card. If your answer is correct, pick up the card. If it was wrong, the card stays on the table. This process is repeated until all the cards are picked up. Once all the cards are up, you should lay the cards out again and repeat the self-test.

When self-testing, if there is a word that you are not sure of, you can peek at the picture to see if it triggers your memory. Since the definition is on the bottom of the card, only turn the card half over, so it cannot be seen. If the picture does not help, then the picture needs to be fixed or changed. Any card peeked at stays on the table until the prompt is not needed.

REFERENCES

Academic Skills Center. (n.d.). *Note taking tips.* California Polytechnic State University, San Luis Obispo, California. Retrieved from http://sas.calpoly.edu/docs/asc/ssl/NoteTakingTips.pdf

Ackerman, D., & Gross, B. (2005). My instructor made me do it: Task characteristics of procrastination. *Journal of Marketing Education, 27*(5), 5–13. doi:10.1177/0273475304273842

Adams, J. (1785). *From John Adams to John Jebb, 10 September 1785.* Retrieved from https://founders.archives.gov/documents/Adams/06-17-02-0232

Aguilar-Roca, N., Williams, A., & O'Dowd, D. (2012). The impact of laptop-free zones on student performance and attitudes in large lectures. *Computers & Education, 59,* 1300–1308.

Alder, M. (1990). Motivation for at-risk students. *Educational Leadership, 48*(1), 27–30.

Ambrose, S., Bridges, M., DiPietro, M., Lovett, M., & Norman, M. (2010). *How learning works: Seven research-based principles for smart teaching.* San Francisco, CA: Jossey-Bass.

American Association of Community Colleges. (2012, April). *Reclaiming the American dream: Community colleges and the nation's future. A report from the 21st-Century Commission on the Future of Community Colleges.* Washington, DC. Retrieved from http://www.aacc21stcenturycenter.org/wp-content/uploads/2014/03/21stCenturyReport.pdf

Angelo, T., & Cross, K. P. (1993). *Classroom assessment techniques* (2nd ed.). San Francisco, CA: Jossey-Bass.

Astin, A. (1999a, Spring). Rethinking academic "excellence." *Liberal Education, 85*(2), 8–18.

Astin, A. (1999b). Student involvement: A developmental theory for higher education. *Journal of College Student Development, 40*(5), 518–529.

Astin, A., & Oseguera, L. (2012). Pre-college and institutional influences on degree attainment. In A. Seidman (Ed.), *College student retention: Formula for student success* (2nd ed., pp. 119–145). Lanham, MD: Rowman & Littlefield.

Bain, K. (2004). *What the best college teachers do.* Cambridge, MA: Harvard University Press.

Baldwin, J. (1995). *Go tell it on the mountain.* New York, NY: The Modern Library.

Bandura, A. (1994). Self-efficacy. In V. S. Ramachandran (Ed.), *Encyclopedia of human behavior* (Vol. 4, pp. 71–81). New York: Academic Press. Retrieved from https://www.uky.edu/~eushe2/Bandura/BanEncy.html

Barkley, E. (2009). *Student engagement techniques: A handbook for college faculty.* San Francisco, CA: Jossey-Bass.

Barone, J. (Ed.). (2016, January 4). A lecture from the lectured. *ChronicleVitae.* Retrieved from https://chroniclevitae.com/news/1235-a-lecture-from-the-lectured

Barr, R., & Tagg, J. (1995, November/December). From teaching to learning—A new paradigm for undergraduate education. *Change, 27*(6), 13–25.

Bean, J. (2001). *Engaging ideas: The professor's guide to integrating writing, critical thinking, and active learning in the classroom.* San Francisco, CA: Jossey-Bass.

Bean, J., & Eaton, S. (2000). A psychological model of college student retention. In J. Braxton (Ed.), *Reworking the student departure puzzle* (pp. 73–89). Nashville, TN: Vanderbilt University Press.

Bean, J., & Eaton, S. (2001–2002). The psychology underlying successful retention practices. *Journal of College Student Retention: Research, Theory & Practice, 3*(1), 73–89.

Beattie, R. (2015). Productive persistence: Tenacity + good strategies: A practical theory of student success. CSU Symposium Speech and PowerPoint slides at Chico, California. Carnegie Foundation for the Advancement of Teaching.

Berger, J., Ramírez, G., & Lyons, S. (2012). Past to present: A historical look at retention. In A. Seidman (Ed.), *College student retention* (2nd ed., pp. 7–34). Lanham, MD: Rowman & Littlefield.

Berk, R. (2002). *Humor as an instructional defibrillator: Evidence-based techniques in teaching and assessment.* Sterling, VA: Stylus.

Berthoff, A. (1981). *The making of meaning: Metaphors, models, and maxims for writing teachers.* Portsmouth, NH: Boynton/Cook.

Blackwell, L. (2002). *You can grow your brain.* Retrieved from http://www.drjessicabc.com/uploads/8/5/9/2/85928276/you_can_grow_your_brain.pdf

Bligh, D. (2000). *What's the use of lectures?* New York, NY: Jossey-Bass.

Bonwell, C., & Eison, J. (1991). Active learning: Creating excitement in the classroom. *1991 ASHE-ERIC Higher Education Reports.* Washington, DC: The George Washington University, School of Education and Human Development. Retrieved from http://files.eric.ed.gov/fulltext/ED336049.pdf

Boyd, D. (n.d.). Using textbooks effectively: Getting students to read them. *Teaching Tips.* Association for Psychological Science. Retrieved from http://www.psychologicalscience.org/teaching/tips/tips_0603.cfm

Bransford, J., Brown, A., & Cocking, R. (Eds.). (2000). *How people learn: Brain, mind, experience, and school.* Washington, DC: National Academies Press.

Braxton, J. (2006, June). *Faculty professional choices in teaching that foster student success.* National Postsecondary Education Cooperative. Retrieved from http://nces.ed.gov/npec/pdf/Braxton_report.pdf

Braxton, J. (2008). Toward a scholarship of practice centered on college student retention. *New Directions for Teaching and Learning, 115,* 101–112. Retrieved from www.interscience.wiley.com. doi:10.1002/tl.328

Braxton, J., Jones, W., Hirschy, A., & Hartley, H., III. (2008, Fall). The role of active learning in college student persistence. *New Directions for Teaching and Learning, 115*, 71–83. doi:10.1002/tl.326

Brockman, E., Taylor, M., Kreth, M., & Crawford, M. (2011). What do professors really say about college writing? *English Journal*. Retrieved from http://www.ncte .org/library/NCTEFiles/Resources/Journals/EJ/1003-jan2011/EJ1003What.pdf

Brookfield, S., & Preskill, S. (2005). *Discussion as a way of teaching: Tools and techniques for democratic classrooms* (2nd ed.). San Francisco, CA: Jossey-Bass.

Buchholz, S., & Ullman, J. (2004, June). 12 commandments for PowerPoint. *Teaching Professor, 18*(6), 4.

Bueschel, A. (2008). *Listening to students about learning*. Strengthening Pre-collegiate Education in Community Colleges (SPECC). Stanford, CA: The Carnegie Foundation for the Advancement of Teaching.

Cadwell, E., & Sorcinelli, M. (1997). The role of faculty development programs in helping teachers to improve student learning through writing. *New Directions for Teaching and Learning, 69*. San Francisco, CA: Jossey-Bass.

Carey, K. (2008). *Graduation rate watch: Making minority student success a priority*. Education Sector Reports. Washington, DC. Retrieved from https://www .issuelab.org/resources/1072/1072.pdf

Carnegie Foundation for the Advancement of Teaching. (n.d.). *Productive persistence*. Retrieved from https://www.carnegiefoundation.org/in-action/carnegie-math-pathways/productive-persistence/

Carnegie Vincent Library. (2013). *Scholarly and popular sources*. Retrieved from https://www.youtube.com/watch?v=tN8S4CbzGXU

Center for Faculty Excellence. (2009, January). *The first day of class: Your chance to make a good first impression*. Chapel Hill, NC: University of North Carolina at Chapel Hill. Retrieved from http://www.unc.edu/tlim/cfe/?First_day_of_class

Centre for Teaching Excellence. (n.d.a). *Low-stakes writing assignments*. University of Waterloo. Retrieved from https://uwaterloo.ca/centre-for-teaching-excellence/ teaching-resources/teaching-tips/developing-assignments/cross-discipline-skills/ low-stakes-writing-assignments

Centre for Teaching Excellence. (n.d.b). *High impact practices (HIPs) or engaged learning practices*. University of Waterloo. Retrieved from https://uwaterloo.ca/ centre-for-teaching-excellence/resources/integrative-learning/high-impact-practices-hips-or-engaged-learning-practices

Chavez, C. (n.d.). AZquotes. Retrieved from www.azquotes.com/author/2761-Cesar_Chavez/

Chickering, A., & Gamson, Z. (1987). Seven principles for good practice in undergraduate education. *Washington Center News, 3–7*. Retrieved from http:// learningcommons.evergreen.edu/pdf/fall1987.pdf

Chickering, A., & Kuh, G. D. (2005). *Promoting student success: Creating conditions so every student can learn* (Occasional Paper No. 3). Bloomington, IN: Indiana University Center for Postsecondary Research.

Churchill, W. (n.d.). BrainyQuote. Retrieved from https://www.brainyquote.com/quotes/quotes/w/winstonchu143691.html

Clough, P., & Strycharczyk, D. (2012a). *Developing mental toughness: Improving performance, wellbeing and positive behaviour in others.* London, England and Philadelphia, PA: Kogan Page Limited.

Clough, P., & Strycharczyk, D. (2012b). Mental toughness and its role in the development of young people. In C. van Nieuwerburgh (Ed.), *Coaching in education: Getting better results for students, educators, and parents* (pp. 75–91). London, England: Karnac Books.

Coates, T.-N. (2015, July/August). There is no post-racial America: The United States needs more than a good president to erase centuries of violence. *Atlantic.* Retrieved from https://www.theatlantic.com/magazine/archive/2015/07/post-racial-society-distant-dream/395255/

Coffman, S. (2009). How to get your students to read what's assigned. In M. Weimer (Ed.), *11 strategies for getting students to read what's assigned.* Faculty Focus Special Report. Madison, WI: Magna Publications. Retrieved from www.facultyfocus.com/free-reports/11-strategies-for-getting-students-to-read-whats-assigned

Colby, A., Ehrlich, T., Beaumont, E., & Stephens, J. (2003). *Educating citizens: Preparing America's undergraduates for lives of moral and civic responsibility.* San Francisco, CA: Jossey-Bass.

Collins, M. (n.d.) AZquotes. Retrieved from http://www.azquotes.com/quote/563910

Copeland, M. (n.d.). *Under armour—Misty Copeland—I will what I want.* Retrieved from https://www.youtube.com/watch?v=zWJ5_HiKhNg

Cornelius, T., & Owen-DeSchryver, J. (2008). Differential effects of full and partial notes on learning outcomes and attendance. *Teaching of Psychology, 35*(1), 6–12.

Cox, R. (2009). *The college fear factor: How students and professors misunderstand one another.* Cambridge, MA: Harvard University Press.

Culver, T., & Morse, L. (2008). Getting students to use their textbooks more effectively. In M. Weimer (Ed.), *11 strategies for getting students to read what's assigned* (pp. 7–8). Faculty Focus Special Report. Madison, WI: Magna Publications. Retrieved from www.facultyfocus.com/free-reports/11-strategies-for-getting-students-to-read-whats-assigned

Cuseo, J. (2010). *What all first-year students should know: The most potent, research-based principles of college success.* Retrieved from https://www.researchgate.net/publication/265011122_What_All_First-Year_Students_Should_Know_The_Most_Potent_Research-Based_Principles_of_College_Success

Davis, B. (n.d.). AZquotes. Retrieved from http://www.azquotes.com/quote/520100

Davis, B. G. (1993). *Tools for teaching.* San Francisco, CA: Jossey-Bass.

Dewey, J. (n.d.). AZquotes. Retrieved from http://www.azquotes.com/quote/502881

Douglass, F. (n.d.). AZquotes. Retrieved from http://www.azquotes.com/author/4104-Frederick_Douglass

Doyle, T. (2008). *Helping students learn in a learner-centered environment: A guide to facilitating learning in higher education.* Sterling, VA: Stylus.

Doyle, T., & Zakrajsek, T. (2013). *The new science of learning: How to learn in harmony with your brain.* Sterling, VA: Stylus Publishing.

Duckworth, A. (2013). *Grit: The power of passion and perseverance.* Retrieved from https://www.ted.com/talks/angela_lee_duckworth_grit_the_power_of_passion_and_perseverance

Duhigg, C. (2012). *The power of habit: Why we do what we do in life and business.* New York, NY: Random House.

Dweck, C. (2006). *Mindset: The new psychology of success.* New York, NY: Penguin Random House.

Dweck, C., & Leggett, E. (1988). A social-cognitive approach to motivation and personality. *Psychological Review, 95*(2), 256–273.

Dweck, C., Walton, G., & Cohen, G. (2014). *Academic tenacity: Mindsets and skills that promote long-term learning.* Bill & Melinda Gates Foundation. Retrieved from https://ed.stanford.edu/sites/default/files/manual/dweck-walton-cohen-2014.pdf

Eberly Center. (2008). *Why are students coming into college poorly prepared to write?* Carnegie Mellon University. Retrieved from www.cmu.edu/teaching/designteach/design/instructionalstrategies/writing/poorlyprepared.html

Eberly Center. (2015). *Explore potential strategies.* Carnegie Mellon University. Retrieved from https://www.cmu.edu/teaching/solveproblem/strat-lackmotivation/lackmotivation-01.html

Eddy, S., & Hogan, K. (2014). Getting under the hood: How and for whom does increasing course structure work? *Life Sciences Education, 13*(3), 453–468. doi:10.1187/cbe.14-03-0050

Edison, T. (n.d.). AZquotes. Retrieved from http://www.azquotes.com/quote/86499

Eli, Q. (1996). *African-American wisdom: A book of quotations and proverbs.* Philadelphia, PA: Running Press Book Publishers.

Engstrom, C. (2008). Curricular learning communities and unprepared students: How faculty can provide a foundation for success. *New Directions for Teaching and Learning, 115,* 5–19. doi:10.1002/tl.322

Feldman, K. (1996). Identifying exemplary teaching: Using data from course and teacher evaluations: Evidence from student ratings. In *New Directions for Teaching and Learning, 65.* San Francisco, CA: Jossey-Bass.

Feldman, K. (2007). Identifying exemplary teachers and teaching: Evidence from student ratings. In R. Perry & J. Smart (Eds.), *The scholarship of teaching and learning in higher education: An evidence-based perspective* (pp. 93–143). New York, NY: Springer.

Fink, D. (2013). *Creating significant learning experiences: An integrated approach to designing college courses.* San Francisco, CA: Jossey-Bass.

Fleming, J. (2012). *Enhancing minority student retention and academic performance: What we can learn from program evaluations.* San Francisco, CA: Jossey-Bass.

Flores, T. (n.d.). AZquotes. Retrieved from http://www.azquotes.com/quote/591470

Franzoi, S., & Ratlif-Crain, J. (2003). *How to read a research study article*. Retrieved from www.cod.edu/library/libweb/blewett/how_to_read_a_research_study_article.doc

Frederick, P. (1995). Walking on eggs: Mastering the dreaded diversity discussion. *College Teaching, 43*(2), 83–92.

Gabriel, K. (1991). *An evaluation of an academic support program for at-risk student-athletes* (Unpublished doctoral dissertation). University of Kansas, Lawrence.

Gabriel, K. (1999a). *Learn the lingo: A strategy for improving your vocabulary, volume I, student manual*. Tucson, AZ: KFG Educational Consultants.

Gabriel, K. (1999b). *Learn the lingo: A strategy for improving your vocabulary, volume I, teacher's manual*. Tucson, AZ: KFG Educational Consultants.

Gabriel, K. (2008). *Teaching unprepared students: Strategies for promoting success and retention in higher education*. Sterling, VA: Stylus.

Gabriel, K. (2016). At-risk and unprepared students in US higher education: The impact on institutions and strategies to address the new student body landscape. In J. E. Cote & A. Furlong (Eds.), *Routledge handbook of the sociology of higher education* (pp. 176–186). New York, NY: Routledge.

Gabriel, K., & Davis, T. (2015, Winter). Implementation of a writing strategy for students with learning disabilities in a rural setting. *Rural Special Education Quarterly, 34*(4), 40–49.

Gehr, K. (2005, January). A global perspective on responding to student writing. *The Teaching Professor, 19*(1), 1–2.

Gorski, P. (2015). *Guide for setting ground rules*. Retrieved from www.edchange.org/multicultural/activities/groundrules.html

Graham, S., & Hebert, M. (2010). *Writing to read: Evidence for how writing can improve reading*. A Carnegie Corporation Time to Act Report. Washington, DC: Alliance for Excellent Education.

Graham, S., & Perin, D. (2007). *Writing next: Effective strategies to improve writing of adolescents in middle and high schools*. A report to Carnegie Corporation of New York. Washington, DC: Alliance for Excellent Education.

Grant, H., & Dweck, C. (2003). Clarifying achievement goals and their impact. *Journal of Personality and Social Psychology, 85*(3), 541–553.

Grant, S. (2000). *Erin Brockovich*. New York, NY: Newmarket Press.

Graunke, S., & Woosley, S. (2005). An exploration of the factors that affect the academic success of college sophomores. *College Student Journal, 39*(2), 367–376.

Grunder, P., & Hellmich, D. (1996). Academic persistence and achievement of remedial students in a community college's success program. *Community College Review, 24*(2), 21–33.

Grunert O'Brien, J., Millis, B., & Cohen, M. (2008). *The course syllabus: A learning-centered approach*. San Francisco, CA: Jossey-Bass.

Habley, W., Bloom, J., & Robbins, S. (2012). *Increasing persistence: Research-based strategies for college student success*. San Francisco, CA: Jossey-Bass.

Halpern, D. (2012, September 21). *Teaching and assessing critical thinking: Helping college students become better thinkers*. Retrieved from http://louisville.edu/ideas-toaction/programs/featured/halpern

Hamer, F. (1964). AZquotes. Retrieved from http://www.azquotes.com/quote/687996

Harris, R. (2015). *Anti-plagiarism strategies for research papers.* VirtualSalt. Retrieved from http://www.virtualsalt.com/antiplag.htm

Hassel, H., & Lourey, J. (2005). The dea(r)th of student responsibility. *College Teaching, 53*(1), 2–13.

Hess, F., Schneider, M., Carey, K., & Kelly, A. (2009). *Diplomas and dropouts: Which colleges actually graduate their students (and which don't).* A Project of the American Enterprise Institute for Public Policy, Washington, DC. Retrieved from http://www.aei.org/paper/100019

Heuberger, B., Gerber, D., & Anderson, R. (1999). Strength through cultural diversity: Developing and teaching a diversity course. *College Teaching, 47*(3), 107–113.

Hobson, E. (n.d.). *Getting students to read: Fourteen tips.* Idea Center: The Excellence in Teaching Center at the University of Georgia Southern University. Retrieved from http://www.ideaedu.org/Portals/0/Uploads/Documents/IDEA%20Papers/IDEA%20Papers/Idea_Paper_40.pdf

Holan, A. (2016, December 13). *2016 Lie of the year: Fake news.* PolitiFact. Retrieved from www.politifact.com/truth-o-meter/article/2016/dec/13/2016-lie-year-fake-news/

Holmes, O. (n.d.). BrainyQuote. Retrieved from https://www.brainyquote.com/quotes/quotes/o/oliverwend386387.html

Huba, M. E., & Freed, J. E. (2000). *Learner-centered assessment on college campuses: Shifting the focus from teaching to learning.* Boston, MA: Allyn & Bacon.

Hughes, L. (n.d.). AZquotes. Retrieved from http://www.azquotes.com/quote/138234

Hurtado, S., Alvarado, A., & Guillermo-Wann, C. (2012). *Inclusive learning environments: Modeling a relationship between validation, campus climate for diversity, and sense of belonging.* Presented at the 2012 Annual Conference of the Association for Studies in Higher Education, Las Vegas, Nevada.

Jaasma, M., & Koper, R. (1999). The relationship of student–faculty out-of-class communication to instructor immediacy and trust and to student motivation. *Communication Education, 48*, 41–47.

Jefferson, T. (1787). *From Thomas Jefferson to Uriah Forrest, with enclosure, 31 December 1787.* Retrieved from https://www.brainyquote.com/quotes/quotes/t/thomasjeff135368.html

Johnson, D., Soldner, M., Leonard, J., Alvarez, P., Inkelas, K., Rowan-Kenyon, H., & Longerbeam, S. (2007). Examining sense of belonging among first-year undergraduates from different racial/ethnic groups. *Journal of College Student Development, 48*(5), 525–542.

Jordan, B. (n.d.). BrainyQuote. Retrieved from https://www.brainyquote.com/quotes/quotes/b/barbarajor383894.html

Jordan, M. (2012). *Michael Jordan "failure" commercial HD 1080p.* Retrieved from https://www.youtube.com/watch?v=JA7G7AV-LT8

Kelly, A., Schneider, M., & Carey, K. (2010). *Rising to the challenge: Hispanic college graduation rates as a national priority*. Washington, DC: American Enterprise Institute for Public Policy. Retrieved from https://www.aei.org/publication/rising-to-the-challenge/

Kiely, E., & Robertson, L. (2016, November 18). *How to spot fake news*. FactCheck.org. Retrieved from http://www.factcheck.org/2016/11/how-to-spot-fake-news/

Kinzie, J., Gonyea, R., Shoup, R., & Kuh, G. (2008). Promoting persistence and success of underrepresented students: Lessons for teaching and learning. *New Directions for Teaching and Learning, 115*. doi:10.1002/tl.323

Klassen, R., Krawchuk, L., & Rajani, S. (2008). Academic procrastination of undergraduates: Low self-efficacy to self-regulate predicts higher levels of procrastination. *Contemporary Educational Psychology, 33*(4), 915–931.

Koebler, J. (2012, April 21). Report: Community college attendance up, but graduation rates remain low. *U.S. News & World Report*. Retrieved from https://www.usnews.com/education/best-colleges/articles/2012/04/21/report-community-college-attendance-up-but-graduation-rates-remain-low

Kolowich, S. (2014, August 11). Can universities use data to fix what ails the lecture? *The Chronicle of Higher Education*. Retrieved from http://www.chronicle.com/article/can-colleges-use-data-to-fix/148307

Kovacs, K. (2016). The state of undergraduate education. *Inside Higher Ed*. Retrieved from https://www.insidehighered.com/news/2016/09/22/more-people-enroll-college-even-rising-price-tag-report-finds

Kuh, G., Cruce, T., Shoup, R., Kinzie, J., & Gonyea, R. (2007). Unmasking the effects of student engagement on first-year college grades and persistence. *The Journal of Higher Education, 79*(5), 540–563.

Kuh, G., Kinzie, J., Buckley, J., Bridges, B., & Hayek, J. (2006, July). *What matters to student success: A review of the literature*. Commissioned Report for the National Symposium on Postsecondary Student Success: Spearheading a Dialog on Student Success. National Postsecondary Education Cooperative. Retrieved from nces.ed.gov/npec/pdf/Kuh_Team_Report.pdf

Kuh, G., Kinzie, J., Buckley, J., Bridges, B., & Hayek, J. (2007). *Piecing together the student success puzzle: Research, propositions, and recommendations*. San Francisco, CA: Jossey-Bass.

Kuh, G., Kinzie, J., Schuh, J., Whitt, E., & Associates. (2005). *Student success in college: Creating conditions that matter*. San Francisco, CA: Jossey-Bass.

Laird, T., Chen, D., & Kuh, G. (2008). Classroom practices at institutions with higher-than-expected persistence rates: What student engagement data tell us. *New Directions for Teaching and Learning, 115*, 85–99. doi:10.1002/tl.327

Laubepin, F. (2013). *How to read (and understand) a social science journal article*. Inter-university Consortium for Political and Social Research, University of Michigan. Retrieved from http://www.icpsr.umich.edu/files/instructors/How_to_Read_a_Journal_Article.pdf

Leamnson, R. (1999). *Thinking about teaching and learning: Developing habits of learning with first-year college and university students*. Sterling, VA: Stylus.

LEARN Center. (2017). *Efficient ways to improve student writing.*. University of Wisconsin, Whitewater. Retrieved from https://www.uww.edu/learn/improving/restiptool/improve-student-writing

Lee, W. (1999). Striving toward effective retention: The effect of race on mentoring African American students. *Peabody Journal of Education, 74*(2), 1–14. Retrieved from http://www.jstor.org/stable/1493074

Light, R. (2001). *Making the most of college: Students speak their minds.* Cambridge, MA: Harvard University Press.

Lincoln, A. (n.d.). AZquotes. Retrieved from http://www.azquotes.com/quote/176083

Locke, J. (n.d.). AZquotes. Retrieved from http://www.azquotes.com/quote/177651

Locks, A., Hurtado, S., Bowman, N., & Oseguera, L. (2008). Extending notions of campus climate and diversity to students' transition to college. *The Review of Higher Education, 31*(3), 257–285.

Longfellow, H. (n.d.). AZquotes. Retrieved from http://www.azquotes.com/quote/178506

Los Angeles Southwest College. (n.d.). *Suggested welcoming openings.* Retrieved from https://1pdf.net/.../suggested-welcome-announcement_5914a4c5f6065dbd44eabc07

Lovett, M. (2013). Make exams worth more than the grade: Using exam wrappers to promote metacognition. In M. Kaplan, N. Silver, D. Lavaque-Manty, & D. Meizlish (Eds.), *Using reflection and metacognition to improve student learning* (pp. 18–52). Sterling, VA: Stylus.

Malcolm X. (n.d.). AZquotes. Retrieved from http://www.azquotes.com/quote/1137367

Mandela, N. (n.d.). AZquotes. Retrieved from http://www.azquotes.com/quote/185308

Marsh, H., & Roche, L. (1997). Making students' evaluations of teaching effectiveness effective. *American Psychologist, 52*(11), 1187–1197.

McBrayer, D. (2001, April). Tutoring systems salvage poor performers. *The Teaching Professor, 15*(4), 3.

McClenney, K. (2004). *Engagement by design: 2004 findings.* Community College Survey of Student Engagement (CCSSE). Retrieved from http://www.ccsse.org/center/resources/docs/publications/2004_National_Report.pdf

McGuire, S. Y. (with McGuire, S.) (2015). *Teach students how to learn: Strategies you can incorporate into any course to improve student metacognition, study skills, and motivation.* Sterling, VA: Stylus.

McKeachie, W. (2001). *McKeachie's teaching tips: Strategies, research, and theory for college and university teachers* (11th ed.). New York, NY: Houghton Mifflin.

McKeachie, W., & Svinicki, M. (2005) *Teaching tips: Strategies, research, and theory for college and university teachers.* Belmont, CA: Wadsworth Publishing.

Menendez, R. (1997). *Stand and deliver.* Woodstock, IL: Dramatic Publishing Company.

Miller, S. (2009). *Validated practice for teaching students with diverse needs and abilities.* Columbus, OH: Pearson Education.

Mills, B. (2012). *Active learning strategies in face-to-face courses.* Idea Paper #53. Retrieved from http://www.ideaedu.org/Portals/0/Uploads/Documents/IDEA%20Papers/IDEA%20Papers/PaperIDEA_53.pdf

Moore, J. (2001). Developing academic warriors: Things that parents, administrators, and faculty should know. In L. Jones (Ed.), *Retaining African Americans in higher education: Challenging paradigms for retaining students, faculty, and administrators* (pp. 70–90). Sterling, VA: Stylus.

Morales, E. (2014). Learning from success: How original research on academic resilience informs what college faculty can do to increase the retention of low socioeconomic status students. *International Journal of Education, 3*(3), 92–102. Retrieved from http://dx.doi.org/10.5430/ijhe.v3n3p92

Mueller, P., & Oppenheimer, D. (2014). The pen is mightier than the keyboard: Advantages of longhand over laptop note taking. *Psychological Science, 25*(6), 1159–1168.

National Center for Education Statistics (NCES). (2012a). *Glossary: Student Right-to-Know Act.* Institute of Education Sciences. Retrieved from https://surveys.nces.ed.gov/ipeds/VisInstructions.aspx?survey=2&id=30084

National Center for Education Statistics (NCES). (2012b, April). *State postsecondary enrollment distributions by race/ethnicity before and after changes to reporting categories: Fall 2004, 2007, and 2010.* Retrieved from https://nces.ed.gov/pubs2012/2012264.pdf

National Center for Education Statistics (NCES). (2015) Demographic and enrollment characteristics of nontraditional undergraduates: 2011–12. Retrieved from https://nces.ed.gov/pubs2015/2015025.pdf

National Center for Education Statistics (NCES). (2016a). Digest of education statistics. Fast facts. Retrieved from https://nces.ed.gov/fastfacts/display.asp?id=98

National Center for Education Statistics (NCES). (2016b). Most current Digest tables. Retrieved from https://nces.ed.gov/programs/digest/current_tables.asp

Neumann, Y., & Neumann, E. (1989). Predicting juniors' and seniors' persistence and attrition: A quality of learning experience approach. *Journal of Experimental Education, 57*(2), 129–140.

Nilson, L. (n.d.). *Getting students to do the readings.* National Education Association. Retrieved from http://www.nea.org/home/34689.htm

Nilson, L. (1998). *Teaching at its best: A research-based resource for college instructors.* Boston, MA: Anker.

Nilson, L. (2014, December 1). Unlocking the mystery of critical thinking. *Faculty Focus.* Retrieved from http://www.facultyfocus.com/articles/instructional-design/unlocking-mystery-critical-thinking/

Noel, J., Forsyth, D., & Kelley, K. (1987). Improving the performance of failing students by overcoming their self-serving attributional biases. *Basic and Applied Social Psychology, 8*(2), 151–162.

Nontraditional Undergraduates: 2011–12. Retrieved from https://nces.ed.gov/pubs2015/2015025.pdf

North Central Texas College Libraries. (2013). *Scholarly journals vs. popular magazines.* Retrieved from https://www.youtube.com/watch?v=2TohbuWsctE

Nowacek, R. (2011). *What makes writing so important?* The Writing Center, Marquette University. Retrieved from http://www.marquette.edu/wac/WhatMakesWritingSoImportant.shtml

Offenstein, J., Moore, C., & Shulock, N. (2010). *Advancing by degrees: A framework for increasing college completion.* Institute for Higher Education Leadership and Policy. Retrieved from http://files.eric.ed.gov/fulltext/ED511863.pdf

Office of Support for Effective Teaching. (2009). *How do I get my students to complete reading assignments?* Albuquerque, NM: The University of New Mexico.

Opp, R. (2002). Enhancing program completion rates among two-year college students of color. *Community College Journal of Research and Practice, 26,* 147–163. doi:10.1080/106689202753385483

Organisation for Economic Co-operation and Development (OECD). (2017). Education at a Glance. Data: Enrolment Rate. Retrieved from https://data.oecd.org/eduatt/enrolment-rate.htm#indicator-chart

Orlando, J. (2013, November 11). Improve your PowerPoint design with one simple rule. *Faculty Focus.* Retrieved from https://www.facultyfocus.com/articles/teaching-with-technology-articles/improve-your-powerpoint-design-with-one-simple-rule/

Paine, T. (n.d.). BrainyQuote. https://www.brainyquote.com/quotes/quotes/t/thomaspain124731.html

Parks, R. (n.d.). AZquotes. Retrieved from http://www.azquotes.com/quote/844221

Pascarella, E., & Terenzini, P. (2005). *How college affects students: A third decade of research, volume 2.* New York, NY: Jossey-Bass.

Paul, A. (2015, September 12). Are college lectures unfair? *New York Times.* Retrieved from https://www.nytimes.com/2015/09/13/opinion/sunday/are-college-lectures-unfair.html

Paul, R., Elder, L., & Bartell, T. (2015). *A brief history of the idea of critical thinking.* (Taken from California Teacher Preparation for Instruction in Critical Thinking: Research Findings and Policy Recommendations: State of California, California Commission on Teacher Credentialing, Sacramento, CA, March 1997). Retrieved from http://www.criticalthinking.org/pages/a-brief-history-of-the-idea-of-critical-thinking/408

Penn State, Teaching and Learning With Technology. (n.d.a). *Plagiarism detection and prevention: An instructor guide.* Retrieved from http://tlt.psu.edu/plagiarism/instructor-guide

Penn State, Teaching and Learning With Technology. (n.d.b). *Why students plagiarize.* Retrieved from http://tlt.psu.edu/plagiarism/instructor-guide/why-students-plagiarize/

Perna, L., & Thomas, S. (2006). *A framework for reducing the college success gap and promoting success for all.* Commissioned Report for the National Symposium on Postsecondary Student Success: Spearheading a Dialog on Student Success. National PostSecondary Education Cooperative. Retrieved from https://nces .ed.gov/npec/pdf/Perna_Thomas_Report.pdf

Pintrich, P. (1999). The role of motivation in promoting and sustaining self-regulated learning. *International Journal of Educational Research, 31,* 459–470.

Price, C. (2013, March). *Motivating students: From apathetic to inspired.* Magna Publications. Retrieved from http://www.magnapubs.com/online-seminars/ motivating-students-from-apathetic-to-inspired-3068-1.html

Purdue Online Writing Lab (OWL). (2013). *Evaluating resources.* Retrieved from https://owl.english.purdue.edu/owl/resource/553/01/

Reason, R., Terenzini, P., & Domingo, R. (2006). First things first: Developing academic competence in the first year of college research in higher education. *Research in Higher Education, 47*(2), 149–175.

Reeves-Cohen, J. (2003). *Roles for discussion of readings.* Unpublished presentation. Eugene Lang College, Eugene, Oregon.

Rendon, L. (2006, October). *Reconceptualizing success for underserved students in higher education.* National Postsecondary Education Cooperative. Retrieved from https://nces.ed.gov/npec/pdf/resp_Rendon.pdf

Reynolds, G. (2008). *Presentation zen: Simple ideas on presentation design and delivery.* Berkeley, CA: New Riders.

Richlin, L. (2006). *Blueprint for learning: Creating college courses to facilitate, assess, and document learning.* Sterling, VA: Stylus.

Roosevelt, F. D. (1938). Address to the National Education Association. Retrieved from http://aboutfranklindroosevelt.com/franklin-delano-roosevelt-quotes/480/

Sadigh, M. (2016, October 10). A simple invitation: Please see me. *Faculty Focus.* Retrieved from http://www.facultyfocus.com/articles/effective-teaching-strategies /simple-invitation-please-see/

Sandeen, C. (2012). High impact educational practices: What we can learn from the traditional undergraduate setting. *Continuing Higher Education Review, 76,* 81–89.

Seidman, A. (2005a). Minority student retention: Resources for practitioners. *New Directions for Institutional Research, 2005*(125), 7–24.

Seidman, A. (2005b). *Retention slide show: Minority student retention: Resources for practitioners.* Center for the Study of College Student Retention. Retrieved from http://cscsr.org/docs/MinorityStudentRetentionResourcesforPractitioners2006 .pdf

Seidman, A. (Ed.). (2012). *College student retention: Formula for student success* (2nd ed.). Lanham, MD: Rowman & Littlefield.

Seymour, E. (2000). Issues and trends: Tracking the processes of change in U.S. undergraduate education in science, mathematics, engineering, and technology. *Science Education, 86*(l), 79–105.

Seymour, E., & Hewitt, N. (1997). *Talking about leaving: Why undergraduates leave the sciences*. Boulder, CO: Westview Press.

Shetterly, M. (2016). *Hidden figures: The American dream and the untold story of the black women mathematicians who helped win the space race*. New York, NY: HarperCollins.

Sleigh, M., Ritzer, D., & Casey, M. (2002). Student versus faculty perceptions of missing class. *Teaching of Psychology, 29*, 53–56.

Social Security Administration. (2015, November). *Education and lifetime earnings*. Retrieved from https://www.ssa.gov/retirementpolicy/research/education-earnings.html

Sperber, M. (2005). How undergraduate education became college lite—and a personal apology. In R. Hersh & J. Merrow (Eds.), *Declining by degrees* (pp. 131–143). New York, NY: Palgrave Macmillan.

Stowe, H. (n.d.). AZquotes. Retrieved from http://www.azquotes.com/quote/285408

Talbert, P. (2012). Strategies to increase enrollment, retention, and graduation rates. *Journal of Developmental Education, 36*(1), 22–36.

Talbert, R. (2014, August 12). Is lecture really the thing that needs fixing? *The Chronicle of Higher Education*. Retrieved from http://www.chronicle.com/blognetwork/castingoutnines/2014/08/12/is-lecture-really-the-thing-that-needs-fixing/

Tatum, B. (1997). *"Why are all the Black kids sitting together in the cafeteria?" And other conversations about race*. New York, NY: Basic Books.

Thompson, B., & Geren, P. (2002). Classroom strategies for identifying and helping college students at risk for academic failure. *College Student Journal, 36*(3), 398–402.

Thompson, M. N. (2013). Native American undergraduate students' persistence intentions: A psychosociocultural perspective. *Cultural Diversity & Ethnic Minority Psychology, 19*(2), 218–228.

Tinto, V. (1997a). Classrooms as communities: Exploring the educational character of student persistence. *The Journal of Higher Education, 68*(6), 599–623.

Tinto, V. (1997b). *Taking student retention seriously*. Speech given to the American Association of Collegiate Registrars and Admission Officers. Retrieved from http://survey.csuprojects.org/uploads/a-/nu/a-nuQmE5d6vFwnkDnNNn7Q/Tinto-re-Taking-Student-Retention-Seriously.pdf

Tinto, V. (2000). Linking learning and leaving: Exploring the role of the college classroom in student departure. In J. Braxton (Ed.), *Reworking the student departure puzzle* (pp. 81–94). Nashville, TN: Vanderbilt University Press.

Tinto, V. (2006–2007). Research and practice of student retention: What next? *Journal of College Student Retention, 8*(1), 1–19.

Tinto, V. (2012). *Completing college: Rethinking institutional action*. Chicago, IL: The University of Chicago Press.

Tinto, V., & Pusser, B. (2006, June). *Moving from theory to action: Building a model of institutional action for student success*. Executive summary. National Postsecondary Education Cooperative, Washington, DC.

University of Oklahoma, Academic Integrity. (n.d.). *Nine things you should already know about plagiarism . . . . Plus six excuses that don't work and . . . three things you don't need to worry about.* Retrieved from http://integrity.ou.edu/files/nine_things_you_should_know.pdf

Vanderbilt University. (2017). *Scholarly vs. popular periodicals.* Retrieved from https://www.youtube.com/watch?v=ysPDZGj3cRA

Veenstra, C. (2009). A strategy for improving freshman college retention. *The Journal for Quality and Participation, 31*(4), 19–23.

Walker, M. (n.d.). AZquotes. Retrieved from http://www.azquotes.com/quote/519998

Wankat, P. (2002). *The effective, efficient professor: Teaching, scholarship and service.* Boston, MA: Allyn & Bacon.

Warren, L. (2002–2006). *Managing hot moments in the classroom.* Derek Bok Center for Teaching and Learning, Harvard University. Retrieved from https://bokcenter.harvard.edu/managing-hot-moments-classroom

Washington, B. (n.d.). AZquotes. Retrieved from http://www.azquotes.com/quote/307628

Wathington, H. (2005). Talking the talk: Rhetoric and reality for students of color. In R. Hersh & J. Merrow (Eds.), *Declining by degrees* (pp. 185–192). New York, NY: Palgrave Macmillan.

Watson, L. W., Terrell, M. C., Wright, D. J., Bonner, F. A. II, Cuyjet, M. J., Gold, J. A., ... Person, D. R. (2002). *How minority students experience college: Implications for planning and policy.* Sterling, VA: Stylus.

Weimer, M. (2002). *Learner-centered teaching: Five key changes to practice.* San Francisco, CA: Jossey-Bass.

Weimer, M. (Ed.). (2010). *11 strategies for getting students to read what's assigned.* Faculty Focus Special Report. Madison, WI: Magna Publications. Retrieved from. www.facultyfocus.com/free-reports/11-strategies-for-getting-students-to-read-whats-assigned

Weimer, M. (2011). *What are the three worst mistakes to make in the classroom?* Magna 20 Minute Mentor. Madison, WI: Magna Publications.

Weimer, M. (2013). How to help students improve their note-taking skills. *The Teaching Professor, 27*(6), 7.

Weimer, M. (2016, August 3). Classroom spaces where great and magical things can happen. *Faculty Focus.* Retrieved from www.facultyfocus.com/articles/teaching-professor-blog/classroom-spaces-great-and-magical-things-can-happen/

Weir, R. (2009, November). They don't read! *Inside Higher Ed.* Retrieved from https://www.insidehighered.com/advice/2009/11/13/they-dont-read

Wood, A. (1998). *The effects of teacher enthusiasm on student motivation, selective attention, and text memory.* Department of Psychology Faculty of Graduate Studies, The University of Western Ontario, London, Ontario.

Wooden, J. (n.d.). AZquotes. Retrieved from www.azquotes.com/quote/320230 and http://www.azquotes.com/quote/320238

Woodson, C. (n.d.). AZquotes. Retrieved from http://www.azquotes.com/quote/1055779

Yeager, D., & Dweck, C. (2012). Mindsets that promote resilience: When students believe that personal characteristics can be developed. *Educational Psychologist,* *47*(4), 302–314. doi:10.1080/00461520.2012.722805

ABOUT THE AUTHOR

Kathleen F. Gabriel is an associate professor at California State University (CSU), Chico, and an educational consultant. She is a nationally recognized author and presenter who has travelled across the United States speaking in more than 30 states promoting effective teaching methods as well as learning strategies for all students, but especially for those who have been traditionally unsuccessful in higher education. She began an extensive teaching career as a high school social science teacher before she became a resource specialist teacher for students with learning disabilities. When moving to the university setting, she first developed an academic support program for at-risk and unprepared college students at the University of Kansas and at the University of Arizona. She also became a faculty development specialist at the University of Arizona, later served as the director of disabled student services at a community college in northern California, and then joined the School of Education at CSU, Chico. She has received several teaching awards throughout her career and her book, *Teaching Unprepared Students: Strategies for Promoting Success and Retention in Higher Education* (Stylus, 2008) has been a best-seller every year since its release. She and her husband live in northern California, enjoying their three children and four grandchildren.

absenteeism, absences, 30, 51
academic challenge, 47, 70, 90, 94,
    121, 122. See also expectations
academic integration, 21, 24, 27, 46,
    122
academic resilience, 115, 118, 124
academic skills centers, 145–146. See
    also tutoring
academic standards, 1, 7, 9, 12, 25,
    49, 59, 111
accountability,
    for institutions, 6
    for students, 65, 66, 67, 82, 87,
Ackerman, D. & Gross, B., 104, 105,
    109
active learning, 11, 35, 63, 64, 67, 70,
    71, 97
activities, see meaningful educational
    activities
Adams, J., 2
admission to college (policies), 7
advisers, 1, 30, 63
    advisory services, 20, 46
Aguilar-Roca, N., Williams, A., &
    O'Dowd, D., 77
Alder, M., 58
Ambrose, S., Bridges, M., DiPietro,
    M., Lovett, M., & Norman, M.,
    35, 37, 75, 106, 107, 117, 118
American Association of Community
    Colleges, 5
Angelo, T., & Cross, K., 37
anxiety, 53, 56, 73
assessments, 121
    formative assessments, 115

assessment skills, 92
Astin & Oseguera, 123
Astin, A., 2, 7, 21, 27, 30, 35, 46, 72,
    78, 80, 130
athletes (student), 22
attendance, habits, 119
attendance, significance of, 32, 120
attention span, 65
attitudes, negative, 59

Background Knowledge Probes, 37
Bain, K., 40, 125
Baldwin, J., 13, 48
Bandura, A., 57, 129
Barkley, E. (2010), 64, 67, 70, 71,
    84, 85
Barone, J., 61
Barr, R. & Tagg, J., 61, 62,
Bean, J. & Eaton, S., 46, 56, 122
Bean, J., 79, 87, 89, 90, 91, 93, 100,
    111
Beattie, R., 47, 49, 50, 121, 122, 123,
    125
Berger, J., Ramirez, G., & Lyons, S.,
    6, 7, 8
Berk, R., 73
bias, 10, 14, 15, 20, 62–64, 92, 111,
    114, 129
Blackwell, 47, 122
Bligh, D., 44, 146,
Bloom's Taxonomy, 69, 70, 84, 97
Bonwell, C. & Eison, J., 97
Boyd, D., 82, 83, 89
Braxton, J., 6, 32, 74, 78, 91, 94,
    120, 127

Braxton, J., Jones, W., Hirschy, A., & Hartley III, H., 35, 78

Brockman, E., Taylor, M., Kreth, M., & Crawford, M., 111,

Brookfield, S. & Preskill, S., 98, 99

Buchholz, S. & Ullman, J., 76

Bueschel, A., 41, 55

busywork, 69

Cadwell, E. & Sorcinelli, M., 97

careers, See future careers

Carey, K., 4, 7, 13

Carnegie Foundation for the Advancement of Teaching, 49, 121, 122, 126

Carnegie Vincent Library, 109

Center for Faculty Excellence. 23, 27, 209

Centers for Teaching, 16, 21, 87, 130. See also faculty development

Centre for Teaching Excellence, 96, 100, 103

challenge, component of mental toughness, 53–54

Chavez, C., 142, 143

cheating, 108, 109

   websites for cheating, 112. See also plagiarism

checklists for writing assignments, 106–107

Chickering, A. & Kuh, G., 61, 62

Chickering, A., & Gamson, Z., 18, 31, 65, 68, 120

Churchill, W., 139

citizenship in a democracy, 2, 3, 92, 96, 127, 130

civic duties, responsibility, 127, 130

class discussions, 30, 100. See also ground rules; small group discussions

class climate, 14, 19, 22, 24, 27, 41, 51, 52, 72, 78, 114, 121, 125–127

class notes, 41, 77, 84, 93, 145–146. See also note-taking tips

class participation, 15, 19, 24, 33, 64, 72, 82, 84, 100

classroom community, 63. See also community of learners

close reader, for small group discussions, 93

Clough, P. & Strycharczyk, D., 51, 52, 53, 55, 56

Coates, T.-N., 131, 142

Coffman, S., 88

Colby, Ehrlich, Beaumont, & Stephens, 2

collaborative and cooperative learning, 24, 63, 68, 71, 93. See also support, student-to-student

Collins, M., 141, 142

commitment, of instructors, 41, 113; of students, 12, 25, 30, 40, 53, 88, 94, 113, 121

   component of mental toughness, 52–53

community of learners, 10, 14, 23, 24, 25, 26, 27, 33, 40, 94, 100, 124

commuters to college, 41,

compensatory effect, 64,

confidence, component of mental toughness, 54–55

connected or connectedness, 15, 21, 32, 35, 36–38, 41, 73, 75, 83–84, 121, 124. See also sense of belonging.

contextualizer, for small group discussions, 93

control, as a component of mental toughness, 55–56

Copeland, M., 55

Cornelius, T., & Owen-DeSchryver, J., 77, 146

Cox, R., 8, 15

critical thinking (applications to the Internet), 92
critical thinking, 11, 93–95, 110–111
cultural competence (improving), 19, 20, 131–133
    cultural context and topics, 14, 21, 39, 40, 83, 84
    cultural tensions, 19. See also multicultural issues, and I am from poem
Culver, T. & Morse, L., 82, 89, 91
Cuseo, J., 87

Davis, B. G., 87
Davis, B., 144
determination, 44, 55, 141, 144
devil's advocate, (for small group discussions), 93
Dewey, J., 95, 144
discrimination, confronting, 15, 18, 21, 84
    responding to a stereotype or racist comment, 34
disengaged (or disengagement), 29, 31, 67, 70, 88, 105, 130
Douglass, F., 131, 132, 143
Doyle, T., 81
Duckworth, A., 56
Duhigg, C., 119, 120, 121
Dweck, C. & Leggett, E., 44, 45, 46, 47
Dweck, C., 45, 46, 49, 50
Dweck, C., Walton, G. & Cohen, G., 46

early signs of academic trouble, 51
Eberly Center, 95, 102, 125
economic ladder, 3
    disparities and inequities, 30
    being self-sufficient, 2
    security, 118

Eddy, S. & Hogan, K., 63, 64, 67, 68, 69, 90
Edison, T., 139
electronic devices (cell phones, laptops, iPads), 31, 32, 94, 146
Eli, Q., 48
e-mail etiquette, 17, 125, 127
    e-mails, student-faculty, 53
Engstrom, C., 5, 38, 64, 126
enthusiasm, from teachers/professors, 40, 72, 74, 130
    boost for students, 12, 15
    lack of, 34, 38
environment of the classroom, see class climate
Eurocentric perspective, 39, 83
    Western civilization views, 100
exams, 63, 69, 82, 112, 116, 147
    essay exams, 96
    exam wrapper, 116–118
expectations of students, 29, 30, 31, 32, 41, 58, 59, 66, 88, 106, 124, 129, 142

facilitator, (for small group discussions), 92
failure (expectations of and overcoming), 12, 44, 45, 47, 54–56, 58, 114, 139
faculty development, 9, 16, 21, 126, 130. See also Center for Faculty Excellence, Center for Teaching, & Centre for Teaching Excellence
fake news, 79, 110
fear factor, 15, 24, 31, 54, 55, 103, 107, 115, 121
federal formula for graduation rates, 4, 5. See also Right-to-Know act/law
feedback, 49, 50, 69, 70, 95, 100, 107

corrective feedback, 11, 25, 111, 102, 124

Feldman, K., 9

financial aid, 1, 63, 80, 125
  financial consequences, 3
  finance problems, 12, 144
  financial sources for websites, 92

freshmen, academic engagement, 30
  academic trouble, 34. See also first-
  year students

fiction books, 132–133. See also
  cultural competence

Fink, D., 83, 100, 101, 103

Fleming, J., 15, 16, 19, 21, 22, 39,
  40, 114, 119, 124, 125

Flores, T., 113

Franzoi, S. & Ratlif-Crain, J., 92

Frederick, P., 38

future careers, 11, 109, 118
  future employment, 3, 32

Gabriel, K. & Davis, T., 95

Gabriel, K., 3, 5, 9, 12, 14, 15, 19,
  21, 25, 35, 41, 54, 58, 66, 68,
  71, 88, 90, 103, 106, 108, 115,
  129, 130, 135

Gehr, K., 104

global perspectives/views, 2, 19, 37,
  39, 83

Gorski, P., 33

graduation gap, 5, 12, 113, 114

graduation rates, 1, 4–7, 11, 16, 41,
  64, 129
  expectations of graduation rates,
  6, 9

Graham, S. & Hebert, M., 11

Graham, S. & Perin, D., 95

Grant, H. & Dweck, C., 45

Grant, S., 87

Graunke, S. & Woosley, S., 34

ground rules,
  for class protocols, 41
  for class discussions, 32–33

for PowerPoints, 75

group learning, students, 22–23, 36,
  37, 61, 67, 85, 99
  ground rules for group
  participation, 32–33
  groups for reading discussions, 92
  stations for group learning 98
  setting up random groups, 135–
  137

Grunder, P., & Hellmich, D., 5, 6,
  44, 126

Grunert O'Brien, J., Millis, B., &
  Cohen, M., 16, 18, 35, 125

guidance from professors, 16, 87, 104,
  129. See also support for
  students

guided-reading questions, 63, 69, 90

habits, characteristics of, 118–121
  habits for lifelong reading, 94
  habits for note-taking, 145
  habits for Productive Persistence,
  125
  rewards that reinforce habits, 119.
  See also routines

Habley, W., Bloom, J. & Robbins, S.,
  1, 3, 4, 6, 9

Halpern, D., 91, 92

Hamer, F., 43, 143, 144

handouts for class notes, 77, 147

Harris, R., 106

Hassel, H., & Lourey, J., 51

help-seeking behaviors, 49, 107, 108,
  115, 121, 122. See also resilience

helpless pattern, 45. See also early
  signs of trouble

Hess, F., Schneider, M., Carey, K. &
  Kelly, A., 4, 7

Heuberger, B., Gerber, D., &
  Anderson, R., 19, 39, 84

high schools, 2,
  writing skills of high school
  students, 95

high-stakes writing assignments, 103, 111. See also writing, substantive and formal

historical events, and/or public figures, 38–39

historically underrepresented groups, 16, 25, 39, 69, 78

Hobson, E., 79, 87, 88, 94

Holan, A., 110

Holmes, O., 140

hot issues, 38

Huba, M., & Freed, J., 104

Hughes, L., 139

humor, 73, 76,

Hurtado, S., Alvarado, A., & Guillermo-Wann, C., 24, 25

I Am From poem, 26. See also cultural competence, multicultural issues

icebreaker, 21, 22

individual, or small group, meetings, see office hours

Integrity Center, University of Oklahoma, 108. See also cheating, plagiarism

intelligence, self-theories about, 44, 45, 47, 122–124. See also Dweck, mindsets, Productive Persistence

intellectual commitment, 121
  dispositions, 127
  efficacy, 129
  intellectually engaging, 126

integration, of students, 21, 27
  social, 24. See also academic integration; connected

inclusion, 19, 20, 33, 39

institutional effectiveness, 6
  efforts, 8
  responsibility, 126

Jaasma, M., & Koper, R., 58

jargon scout, (for small group discussions), 93

Jefferson, T., 2

jobs and training (American), 2, 3

Johnson et al., 98, 124

Jordan, B., 1, 141

Jordan, M., 55

Kelly, A., Schneider, M., & Carey, K., 14

key points,
  in lectures, 77, 147
  in readings, 87. See also guided-reading questions

Kiely, E., & Robertson, L., 110

Kinzie, J., Gonyea, R., Shoup, R., & Kuh, G., 23

Klassen, R., Krawchuk, L., & Rajani, S., 44

knowledge, prior, See prior knowledge

Koebler, J., 3

Kolowich, S., 62, 75

Kuh, G., Cruce, T., Shoup, R., Kinzie, J., & Gonyea, R., 64

Kuh, G., Kinzie, J., Buckley, J., Bridges, B., & Hayek, J., 3, 5, 7, 8, 30, 38, 58, 72, 88, 58, 116, 124

Kuh, G., Kinzie, J., Schuh, J., Whitt, E., and Associates, 22, 23, 25, 36, 37, 99

Laird, T., Chen, D. & Kuh, G., 30, 59, 91, 102, 113, 118, 120, 127

language,
  body, 33
  inappropriate, 34, 73

Laubepin, E., 92

Leamnson, R., 81

Learn Center (University of Wisconsin, Whitewater), 98, 104

Learn the Lingo: A Strategy for Building a Better Vocabulary, 149–151 learner-centered teaching, 12, 23, 32, 66

learning communities, 23. See also community of learners

learning outcomes (or objectives), 9, 52, 121,

lectures, interactive, 61–78

Lee, W., 3, 7

letters of recommendation, 32. See also future careers

lifelong learning, 78, 94, 127

Light, R., 34, 104

Lincoln, A., 140

Locke, J., 79

Locks, A., Hurtado, S., Bowman, N., & Oseguera, L., 14, 25

Longfellow, H., 140

Los Angeles Southwest College, 16

Lovett, M., 116, 117

low-stakes writing assignments, 11, 100, 111, 115

Malcolm, X., 29

Mandela, N., 144

Marsh, H. & Roche, L., 9

McBrayer, D., 116

McClenney, K., 2, 4, 53

McGuire, S., 81, 69

McKeachie, W., 31, 33, 34, 39

meaningful connections, 39. See also connections, and sense of belonging

meaningful educational activities, 61, 62, 64, 65, 68–70, 72, 78, 97, 101, 124

memory, 36, 74, 149–151

Menendez, R., 53

Mental Toughness Assessment (MTQ48), 59
aspects of, 50–56, 59

metacognition, 69, 116

Miller, S., 95

Mills, B., 72, 97

misconception-preconception check, 37. See also prior-knowledge

mindsets (fixed and growth), 44–50, 59. See also Productive Persistence

Moore, J., 18

Morales, E., 13, 96, 102, 103, 107, 115, 118

motivation, 14, 29, 34–35, 38, 43–59, 62, 68–69, 72, 74, 85, 102, 121–122, 123–125

Mueller, P. & Oppenheimer, D., 77, 146, 147

multicultural issues, content, 20, 21, 39, 40, 84, 100. See also cultural competence

multicultural training for faculty, 21. See also faculty development

nameplates, 23

names, learning students' names, 21–23
using students' names in class, 25, 123

National Center for Education Statistics, 3, 4, 13

Neumann, Y., & Neumann, E., 34

Nilson, L., 50, 81, 82, 89, 91

Noel, J., Forsyth, & Kelley, K., 51

nonfiction books and articles, 131–132. See also cultural competence

North Central Texas College Libraries, 109

note-taking tips for students, 77, 145–146. See also class notes

notetaking, how professors can help, 146–147

Nowacek, R., 96

Nuhfer, E., Humbolt State, 36

Offenstein, J., Moore, C., & Shulock, N., 5

office hours, 53, 54, 90, 123
Office of Support for Effective
    Teaching, University of New
    Mexico, 87, 88
Opp, R., 5, 7, 18, 25
Orlando, J., 76,

Paine, T., 140, 141
Palmer, Parker, 38
Parks, R., 61
Pascarella, E. & Terenzini, P., 35,
    113, 116
Paul, A., 64,
Paul, R., Elder, L. & Bartell, T., 91
peer-reviewed journals or resources,
    31, 92, 96, 109, 110
peer support, see support, student-to-
    student
Penn State Teaching and Learning
    With Technology, 108
Perna, L. & Thomas, S., 1
pictures (photos),
    of diverse learners, 57
    of diverse professionals
    of graduation, 58
    for PowerPoints, 76. See also
        vocabulary strategy
Pintrich, P., 84, 93
plagiarism, 11, 78, 95, 103, 108–109,
    112. See also cheating, & You Be
    the Judge
PowerPoints, 11, 62, 75–76, 145
predominantly White institutions
    (PWIs), 18–19, 25, 57
Price, C., 66, 68
prior knowledge, 29, 35–37, 42,
    70, 150
privileged populations, 64
procrastination, 95, 103–105
Productive Persistence 49, 114,
    121–122, 124, 125, 126
Purdue Online Writing Lab (OWL),
    110, 127

quote of the week examples, 139–144
quizzes, 83, 147, 149

Race: The power of an illusion, 133
real world issues, 29, 37–38, 47,
    68, 83, 118, 125, 139. See also
    relevancy
Reason, R., Terenzini, P., and
    Domingo, R., 63, 120, 127
reading difficulties, 88–90. See also
    vocabulary building strategy,
    roles (for reading & class
    discussions)
Reeves-Cohen, J., 92, 93
reflections/responses, 67, 83, 102,
    111, 121, 143
    on class notes, 77
    on exam performance, 116
    on readings, 47, 84–86, 88. See
        also writing assignments, exam
        wrapper
relevancy of course and content, 10,
    29, 34, 35, 37–38, 40, 43, 68,
    83, 87, 90, 125
    class activities, 68. See also cultural
        context and real world issues
Rendon, L., 24, 84, 92, 93, 100, 127
resilience, 107, 124. See also academic
    resilience
responsibility for learning, 83, 93, 96,
    98, 113
    for reaching out, 12, 114
    for promoting civic engagement, 130
    for increasing cultural competence,
        14
    for giving lectures, 61
    for acquiring the textbooks and
        reading, 79
    for faculty development 126
Reynolds, G., 75, 76
Richlin, L., 122
Right-to-Know act/law, 4–6
rigor (academic), 25, 35, 39, 64. See
    also academic standards

roles (for reading and class
     discussions), 92–93
Roosevelt, F. D., 2
rotating stations, 98–100
routines, 118–121
rubrics, for writing assignments, 104,
     106

Sadigh, M., 54
Sandeen, C., 104
scholarly versus popular periodicals
     videos, 109
Seidman, A., 3, 5, 6, 127
self-defeating behavior, 51, 59
self-efficacy, 43, 44, 56–59, 103, 115,
     123, 129
self-reflection, 116
   on cultural competence, 20, 14
   self-awareness, 97
   self-appraisal, 115
sense of belonging, 14, 24, 25, 27, 84.
     See also connectedness
Seymour, E., 44, 46
Seymour, E., & Hewitt, N., 46, 54
Shetterly, M., 83
Sleigh, M., Ritzer, D., & Casey, M., 58
small groups for group-work, 22, 99
   for class discussions, 32
   setting-up groups, 135–137. See
     also roles (for reading and class
     discussions) and rotating stations
Social Security Office of Retirement
     Policy, 3
socioeconomic status, 5, 7, 13, 18,
     96, 107
Sperber, M., 62
standardized graduation rates, See
     Right-to-Know act/law
standards, See academic standards
Stowe, H., 139
support for students (from professors
     and staff), 25, 27, 31, 37, 114,
     122

support of public schools, 2
support, students-to-students, 122,
     124
supporting growth mindsets, 55,
     139–144
syllabus, 14, 16, 18, 24, 31, 32, 79,
     81, 88, 101. See also welcome
     message

taking class notes, see class notes, and
     note-taking tips
Talbert, P., 123
Talbert, R., 62
Tatum, B., 25, 26. See also I Am
     From poem
teaching philosophy, 16
tests, preparing for, 30
   improving performances, 54
   inclusion of culturally relevant
     material, 39–40
   self-test, 151. See also exams
textbooks, 30, 36, 39, 41, 70, 71, 72,
     75, 80–91, 119, 149
   on reserve in the library, 94
Thompson, B. & Geren, P., 51
Thompson, MN., 31, 124
Tinto, V. & Pusser, B., 8
Tinto, V., 1, 3, 6, 7, 13, 21, 23, 24,
     27, 30, 34, 41, 46, 54, 58, 61,
     64, 126
traditional lectures, 61–64. See also
     bias
tutoring, 6, 103, 107. See also
     Academic Skills Centers

University of New Mexico, Office of
     Support for Effective Teaching,
     87, 88
University of Oklahoma, Integrity
     Center, 108
University of Waterloo, Centre for
     Teaching Excellence, 96, 100,
     103

University of Wisconsin, Whitewater,
    LEARN Center, 98, 104
usefulness of course, see relevancy

validation, 24, 25, 126
Vanderbilt University, scholarly versus
    popular periodicals, 109
Veenstra, C., 44
vocabulary building strategy,
    149–151
vulnerable students, 9, 45, 113

Walker, M., 47, 48
Wankat, P., 65
Warren, L., 38
Washington, B., 144
Wathington, H., 18
Watson, L., Terrell, M., Wright, D., &
    Associates, 16, 19, 20

Weimer, M., 4, 14, 15, 16, 81, 83, 90,
    96, 104, 114, 116, 117, 147
Weir, R., 86,
welcome climate, 14, 16, 19, 33
    welcome messages, 14, 17, 18, 25
Wood, A., 72, 73, 74
Wooden, J., 140,
Woodson, C., 141
worst mistake teachers can make, 114
writing assignments, low-stakes,
    100–101, 111
    high-stakes, 101–102, 111
    free-writes, 97–98

Yeager, D. & Dweck, C., 115, 122,
    124
You Be the Judge (of plagiarism)
    activity, 112
You Can Grow Your Brain, 47, 122

Of course, every student is an individual. But they are individuals whose behavior can tell us much if we will seek for the patterns and pull in from disparate disciplines the wisdom that bears on their choices and motivations. Tolman and Kremling tell the stories to find the patterns, and give us an apparatus for solving the problems rather than just blaming the students."
—*John Tagg, Associate Professor of English, Palomar College, and co-author with Robert B. Barr of the seminal article "From Teaching to Learning"*

The purpose of this book is to help faculty develop a coherent and integrated understanding of the various causes of student resistance to learning, providing them with a rationale for responding constructively, and enabling them to create conditions conducive to implementing effective learning strategies.

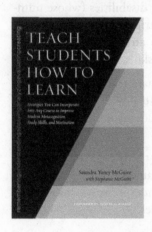

Teach Students How to Learn

Strategies You Can Incorporate Into Any Course to Improve Student Metacognition, Study Skills, and Motivation

Saundra Yancy McGuire with Stephanie McGuire

Foreword by Thomas Angelo

"This book is a wonderful resource for college faculty. It provides us with practical, yet powerful, learning strategies and metacognition techniques that can be easily incorporated into our courses, and which in turn, will improve student learning. McGuire shares both research and her personal experiences, as well as her expertise in teaching all kinds of diverse students with tremendous success. This book is a welcome addition for the postsecondary teaching and learning field and should be read and utilized by all."—*Kathleen F. Gabriel, Associate Professor, School of Education, California State University, Chico*

What is preventing your students from performing according to expectations? Saundra McGuire offers a simple but profound answer: If you teach students how to learn and give them simple, straightforward strategies to use, they can significantly increase their learning and performance.

22883 Quicksilver Drive
Sterling, VA 20166-2102   Subscribe to our e-mail alerts: www.Styluspub.com

Also available from Stylus

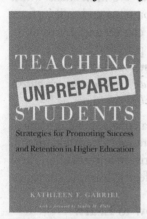

Teaching Unprepared Students

Strategies for Promoting Success and Retention in Higher Education

Kathleen F. Gabriel

Foreword by Sandra M. Flake

As societal expectations about attending college have grown, professors report increasing numbers of students who are unprepared for the rigors of postsecondary education—not only more students with learning disabilities (whose numbers have more than tripled) but also students (with and without special admission status) who are academically at risk because of inadequate reading, writing, and study skills.

This book provides professors and their graduate teaching assistants—those at the front line of interactions with students—with techniques and approaches they can use in class to help at-risk students raise their skills so that they can successfully complete their studies.

The author shares proven practices that will not only engage all students in a class but also create the conditions—while maintaining high standards and high expectations—to enable at-risk and underprepared students to develop academically and graduate with good grades.

Why Students Resist Learning

A Practical Model for Understanding and Helping Students

Edited by Anton O. Tolman and Janine Kremling

Foreword by John Tagg

"This is not the first book to address student resistance. However, as far as I can tell, it is the first book to address the phenomenon systematically and in a way that brings together a variety of perspectives and disciplines that can help to explain it . . . [and] that integrates what we know about psychology, pedagogy, and learning science to construct a framework for recognizing, diagnosing, and addressing such resistance.

(Continues on preceding page)